BRADBURY
An Illustrated Life

BRADBURY
An Illustrated Life

A JOURNEY TO FAR METAPHOR

JERRY WEIST

Foreword by Donn Albright

Introduction by Ray Bradbury

WILLIAM MORROW

An Imprint of HarperCollins*Publishers*

HarperCollins books may be purchased for educational, business, or sales promotional use.
For information please write: Special Markets Department, HarperCollins Publishers Inc.,
10 East 53rd Street, New York, NY 10022.

FIRST EDITION

Designed by Betty Lew

Printed on acid-free paper

Library of Congress Cataloging-in-Publication Data
Weist, Jerry.
Bradbury : an illustrated life : a journey to far metaphor / Jerry Weist.— 1st ed.
p.   cm.
ISBN 0-06-001182-3
1. Bradbury, Ray, 1920–   2. Authors, American—20th century—Biography.
3. Science fiction—Authorship.   I. Title
PS3503.R167 Z93   2002
813'.54—dc21
[B]   2002021913

02   03   04   05   06   ❖/TP   10   9   8   7   6   5   4   3   2   1

CONTENTS

This book is dedicated with love to my immediate family—

Alice, Lenore, Eric, Ian, and Dana,

and to my metaphorical fantastical family—

Donn Albright, Forry Ackerman, and Ray and Maggie Bradbury

FOREWORD
by Donn Albright

I t's a black Los Angeles evening in October. The Bradbury home is dark, except for one dim light in the dining room. There, huddled like a giant troll, sits Ray, chuckling. He is brandishing one of many markers strewn about a cluttered table that would do justice to the Collyer brothers. He's revising the color sketch sent to him for a new edition of *Graveyard for Lunatics*.

"This is what the damn cover should look like! Look what they sent me! It's all wrong. It has nothing to do with the book!"

I sit down as he doodles out a series of headstones with busts atop them. Together, we think up Hollywood personalities for each one. Gleefully he adds a final flourish of loops to represent dangling spools of film. "Wah-la . . ."

Nine months later the new edition is out. Ray's sketch was used as a guide for the final HarperPerennial illustration . . . and it looks great! I should stress that Ray has done this often, starting with his first collection, *Dark Carnival*.

Fred Banbery and I shared the same agent in the mid-sixties. I told him how much I loved his drawing for "The Window" in *Collier's* magazine. Banbery smiled. "You know I'll

Donn Albright and Jerry Weist pose with *The Illustrated Man* movie statue at the Albright archives, spring 2001. Photograph by Tom Warren (© Tom Warren, 2001)

always be indebted to Bradbury. That picture inspired *Collier's* to commission me to illustrate the five-part serial for John Wyndham's *Revolt of the Triffids*." (It should be noted that this magazine serialization appeared months before its release as a Doubleday science fiction novel, *The Day of the Triffids*.) Banbery did wonderful line and watercolor illustrations.

The September 1954 issue of *Cosmopolitan* magazine printed "The Swan." Al Parker, the most respected and imitated illustrator of the fifties, did the art. He illustrated every story in that issue, selecting a different style and alias for each. He'd previously done Ray's "The World the Children Made" and "The Whole Town's Sleeping" for the slicks.

When I told Stanley Meltzoff how much I admired his painting for "The Illustrated Man" in *Esquire,* he remarked, "That was when Bradbury and I worked for $150.00 a page!" I said I thought his characterization of the unsavory, obese tattooed man was wonderful. "Ah, yes . . . that was my brother-in-law." He grinned.

Anthony Saris and I taught illustration together for twenty-five years. His first big break after World War II was illustrating "The Season of Disbelief" for *Collier's*. Eight years ago, he dug that painting out of storage and presented it to me. I'd loved that picture since I first saw it in 1950.

Ben Shahn's powerful drawing for "The Season of Sitting," from *Charm,* is part of the permanent collection of the Museum of Modern Art in New York City. Shahn illustrated two other Bradbury stories for *Charm* and *Esquire.*

In your hands you hold not only a history of Ray Bradbury for the last eight decades, but also a history of editorial art during the past sixty years. The giants of picture-making have illustrated his work, from Hannes Bok and Lee Brown Coye all the way to Charles Addams. Frank Frazetta, Tomi Ungerer, James Bama, Al Hirschfeld, Doris Lee, the Dillons, Edward Gorey, Folon, and, yes, Picasso have visualized his unique worlds.

As beautifully recorded here by Jerry Weist, this mutual love affair of words and pictures, author and artists is inspiring.

—Westfield, New Jersey
January 2002

Preface

Ever since the beginning of my friendship with Ray Bradbury I have sent him books. I first wrote to him in 1968, during my second year of college. To my surprise, he replied immediately. And so began a wonderful friendship, forged through our written correspondence, and our mutual exchanges of books. Once I found a rare, early turn-of-the-century French *Circus* hardcover; knowing of Ray's love for the circus, I sent it to him. There have been books of magic, rare comic volumes, and other treasures, all of which I've sent his way. Many times I've sent my own copies of Ray's books, and asked him to sign and return them to me.

I tried three times during the 1970s to meet Ray. Each time I made it to Los Angeles and events would conspire against our meeting (once his basement was flooded). Through it all we continued our pen pal relationship. It wasn't until the summer of 1993 that Ray and I finally met face-to-face, in Washington, D.C. We recently joked that I had to come up with an idea for an important Bradbury book to finally spend time with him in his home!

Since I live in Massachusetts and he in California, we rarely see each other. My best memory is of when I sent three of my most prized first editions (including *The Illustrated Man*) to Ray. This time I asked him to do color drawings inside the copies that he was signing and returning to me. The package also included a few rare books and a couple of sketches by Hannes Bok: gifts for Ray. My wife (we were newly married) found out, and was shocked. "You asked Ray Bradbury to do original drawings in your books? How presumptuous!"

Two days later the pre-addressed Federal Express box returned, and in triumph I opened it in front of my wife to reveal three signed books. Inside *The Illustrated Man* was a beautiful multicolored Illustrated Man signed, "From

The Illustrated Man Himself, To Jerry Weist." A short accompanying letter said: "Dear Jerry: Send more books! Send more Boks! Love, Ray."

"What is a Bok?" my wife asked. To those who do not what a Bok is, I say read the first chapter of this book. And to *everyone* who has picked up this book, I say, here is my selfish gift to you. "Selfish" because I have always fantasized about just such a book as this, and many times I have imagined myself poring over and enjoying a "visual history" of the author whom I love most.

Jerry Weist and Donn Albright pose with *The Illustrated Man* movie statue at the Albright archives, spring 2001. Photograph by Tom Warren (© Tom Warren, 2001)

Part of the joy of building the chapters to *Bradbury: An Illustrated Life* was making discoveries about Ray's life. The original 1950s letters written to Bill Gaines during Ray's period with EC comics were a revelation. Reviewing François Truffaut's diary notes in *Cahiers du Cinéma* made me realize that we (most of us) had all but forgotten the effort that went into this unique film. Seeing for the first time some of Ray's own paintings, and Joseph Mugnaini's original gel (theater) paintings, sent shivers of delight down my spine. Ray loaned me (even if just for short time) the original volume of *Once Upon a Time* that his Aunt Neva read to him when he was a child. All of this and more made me realize how lucky we are to have an author who remembers and treasures well into his adult life the simple joys of childhood that most of us have forgotten.

Ray himself provided the subtitle, *A Journey to Far Metaphor,* to this book. As he has said many times, his entire life has been, and continues to be, a search for metaphors through his writing. After reviewing this book's images and text, Ray told me it is a volume of "visual metaphors." It is. And it is much more, for this book also tells the story of the growth of popular culture in America during the second half of the twentieth century.

Bradbury: An Illustrated Life is arranged by chapters, highlighting the themes and concerns of Ray Bradbury's life, put forward for you to absorb, and enjoy, and remember. Perhaps it will help you recall your own childhood, and in doing so open fresh pages in the book that is still becoming your own life.

And so I present this book to you, and like the books that I used to send to Ray Bradbury, I am, with the help of many other people, sending this volume out into the larger world. It is for everyone to enjoy. My hope is that you will discover (as I have discovered) the vast, wide, and wonderful world that Bradbury has given us.

—Jerry Weist,
Gloucester, Massachusetts
January 2002

ACKNOWLEDGMENTS

When the idea for *Bradbury: An Illustrated Life* first began to take form, I immediately wrote to two individuals: Ray Bradbury and Donn Albright. I was keenly aware of what an arduous task such a project represented, and knew that it would be essential to call on Bradbury's archivist and friend, Donn Albright. Ray Bradbury would also have to give his blessing and aid in the search for "visual metaphors." Thus two letters were sent on the same day.

I received Donn's response first, pledging his support. Shortly thereafter Ray himself gave me his blessing.

The backbone of this book owes its debt to Donn Albright, who shared his vast collection, files, and memory with me. And, in the summer of 2001, during a visit to Bradbury's summer home, Donn noticed the condition of the original painting by Joseph Mugnaini, done for the May 1963 issue of *The Magazine of Fantasy and Science Fiction*. He did both Ray and me another favor by cleaning and restoring the original that would ultimately become the cover art for this book!

It's also worth noting that I spent many an hour devouring the pages of *The Ray Bradbury Companion*, a wonderful book by author and close Bradbury associate William F. Nolan. This volume played no small part in inspiring *Bradbury: An Illustrated Life*.

Ray and Maggie Bradbury have been gracious, kind, and patient. They've opened their home to me, assisted me in locating documents and artwork, and allowed photography of the paintings in their private collection. Ray Bradbury has also contributed his own magical paintings and writing to this volume.

Patrick Kachurka, Mr. B's personal driver, was a model of consideration, assistance, and charm during my Los Angeles trip to the Bradbury home. God bless him.

Of course, many people aided me in the research and work this book entailed. Tom Warren made the trip to the Midwest to photograph the Albright collection, and then spent time in Los Angeles photographing the Bradbury collection, aspects of the Mugnaini estate, and costumes from the Colony Theater. Tom's expert photography graces page after page in this book.

Glynn Crain sustained me with ideas, loaned me images from his collection, and accompanied me to Los Angeles to help in the "dig" for visual metaphors. Glynn also photographed the series of Bradbury "hands" that open each chapter.

Alice Lewis took on the role of my assistant throughout the summer and fall of 2001, helping with computer work, initial design layouts (chapter three, and chapters five through eight), research, and editing skills. Her help was invaluable.

Forrest J Ackerman gave me access to his personal files, loaned me images, and wrote about his time with Ray Bradbury.

Benard Mahe helped me contact Quardia Teraha at *Cahiers du Cinéma* and procure permission to use the Truffaut diary notes for the filming of *Fahrenheit 451.*

Barbara Beckley of the Colony Theater in Los Angeles aided me with specific information about Bradbury plays, photographs, and costumes; thanks to her, the theater chapter came into full focus.

Wendy Gaines Bucci, Cathy Gaines Mifsud, Chip Selby, Dave Winiewicz, Dorthy Crouch, and Jack Albert all contributed to the chapter on EC Comics. A special thanks goes to Wendy Gaines Bucci who permitted me to use the Bill Gaines letters to Ray Bradbury. The author also wishes to thank Al Feldstein for use of his original paintings and his interview for the EC chapter. Barbara Boatner graciously allowed use of her photographs for the EC chapter. Ellie Frazetta kindly gave permission for the use of the original Frank Frazetta oil paintings for the EC Ballantine paperback reprints. Russ Cochran gave permission for the use of William Mason's writing about the artwork of Berni Krigstein.

Ron and Margaret Borst loaned transparencies from their collection, and welcomed photographer Tom Warren into their home for a special shoot of Bradbury film material. Eric Spilker of Photofest in New York helped me find rare Bradbury TV and film photographs. Peter Gutkowski did timely restoration to rare SF covers for the first chapter. Stuart Schiff contributed the unused Bradbury cover to *Whispers* by Gahan Wilson. Dennis Kitchen loaned rare Buck Rogers proof sheets pictured in chapter one. Mel Korshak allowed image use of *Let's Ride a Rocket,* an unpublished anthology from the 1950s. Danton Burroughs gave permission for use of images from Edgar Rice Burroughs's novels and comics. Robert Weinberg and Victor Dricks kindly granted permission to use images from *Weird Tales*. Steve Kennedy loaned letters and photographs from the estate of Hannes Bok. Byron Preiss gave permission for images from *The Ray Bradbury Chronicles,* and wrote a short historical note. Adtech Photolab in San Antonio provided last-minute color transparencies. Doug Ellis allowed the use of the rare early 1939 Worldcon photos from the Jack Darrow estate. Julie Schwartz aided in advice for the first chapter. Hugh Hefner and Marcia Terrones graciously assisted the author with permissions from *Playboy* illustrations. Bob Madle wrote the early history of Bradbury at the 1939 Worldcon. Frank Robinson helped inspire and advise the early formation of this book. Andre Norton wrote a short visual metaphor about Bradbury. Jane Frank helped me procure permissions from Jim Burns, Ian Miller, and Michael Whelan for the use of their original artwork for Bradbury books. Robert Wiener gave me important advice, and Michaela Nastasia helped with last-minute design work, research, and photographic alterations to Colony costume backgrounds. Reed Orenstein coordinated last-minute logistics with HarperCollins, and gave me important assistance.

I am extremely grateful to Tee Addams, widow of Charles Addams, and H. Kevin Miserocchi, trustee of the Tee and Charles Addams Foundation, who graciously permitted me to include Charles Addams's painting created for Ray's 1946 story "Homecoming."

I owe a special thanks to Diana Robinson, the daughter of Joseph Mugnaini. Diana contributed original artwork from the Mugnaini estate, shared previously unknown originals from *Icarus Motgolfier Wright,* and gave permissions for the use of artwork and photographs. The memory of her father's special relationship with Ray Bradbury is enhanced by her contributions.

Finally I am indebted to my agent, Lori Perkins. Lori never gave up on the idea of *Bradbury: An Illustrated Life,* and without her experience and help this book would never have happened. I have also been blessed with the talents of my editor, Jennifer Brehl; her assistant, Devi Pillai; and the excellent Betty Lew, who as design manager created the book that you now hold in your hands.

INTRODUCTION:
Journey to Far Metaphor
by Ray Bradbury

I don't think the word *metaphor* ever entered my life until twenty years ago.

I was producing my *The Martian Chronicles* on stage at the El Rey Theater in Los Angeles while, six blocks away, at the Los Angeles County Art Museum, there was a display of treasures from King Tutankhamen's tomb. During a rehearsal break one evening I walked to the museum, stood over the glorious golden mask of Tutankhamen. I stared at it for a long moment and cried, "My God! That's one of my Martians!"

Back at the theater I stared at all my actors dressed in their Martian costumes, wearing golden masks and cried, "My God! It's Tutankhamen!"

So I realized I'd been saving King Tut metaphors, seen in newspapers when I was three, and now reborn on stage here in Los Angeles. This made me review my life, to find more images collected from the age of three onward.

It began with seeing *The Hunchback of Notre Dame* and, a few years later, *The Phantom of the Opera* and *The Lost World,* with its superb dinosaurs. The images in these movies stunned me with their simplicity and their drama.

When I was seventeen I saw *The Hunchback of Notre Dame* again, with friends. Before entering the theater I told them that I remembered this scene, and that scene—I remembered the film almost entirely.

Jerry Weist with Ray Bradbury in Bradbury's California home, October 2001

My friends laughed at me, saying that it was impossible to remember a film I'd seen only once, when I was three!

In the theater we saw *The Hunchback* and there it all was, exactly as I had described it.

The same thing happened with *The Phantom of the Opera* and the dinosaurs in *The Lost World*. The metaphors were so powerful that they changed my life. I began collecting metaphors without knowing it. I still do so, to this day.

When I was seven Blackstone came to the Genesee Theater in Waukegan. What first attracted me was a gigantic poster on the side of the theater, which stood across the street from the school where I attended the second grade. I was immediately transfixed the moment I first saw that incredible poster. I stood there for an hour, feeding on those wild images of mystery and magic.

That's when I made up my mind that I wanted to move on the stage with such miracles, to cause elephants to disappear and Arabian horses to manifest. I began to collect posters filled with illusions.

When I was nine years old, Buck Rogers arrived—a super metaphor. That one stupendous strip in October 1929 exploded me into the future.

Dick Calkins, the first *Buck Rogers* daily from October 1929. Framed with the inscription "Our Only Boundaries Are Our Dreams," a reproduction of the illustration was given to Ray Bradbury by a loving fan. (Courtesy of the collection of Ray Bradbury)

I threw myself into tomorrow and never returned, collecting Buck Rogers comic strips, collecting metaphors.

My school chums laughed at me so I tore the strips up. But soon, weeping at how foolish I had been, I started collecting them again.

When I was twelve I met Mr. Electrico and his traveling carnival. He sat in an electric chair to be electrocuted every night. I went to see him, carrying a metaphor in my pocket, a magic trick I couldn't quite work. I held it out in the palm of my hand and asked Mr. Electrico to do it.

It was at that encounter that he told me to live forever. When I left the carnival grounds I stood by the carousal and watched the horses spinning to the calliope music of "Beautiful Ohio." Tears ran down my face because I knew something amazing had happened. I had met a magician and was to become a magician.

Within weeks of that epiphany I began to write my first stories about Mars, that planet I had known from the books of Edgar Rice Burroughs. In high school, my stories multiplied while I collected and created metaphors without realizing it.

My first successful story, in *Super Science,* was a super metaphor. A man, accused of criminal acts, was imprisoned in a giant pendulum which swung back and forth, causing him to serve time and to move in time simultaneously.

As my stories appeared over the years the Hunchback, the Phantom, and the *Lost World* dinosaurs surged into my life.

In my thirties I wrote *The Illustrated Man* and realized that he was one of the freaks I had met behind the scenes with Mr. Electrico when I was twelve. Late nights, when he perspired, all the images on his body came forth. So the images in my own life, as I perspired over my typewriter, rose up. I finished the story and suddenly it became a book.

Images were always inspiring me. In high school I found old copies of *Coronet* magazine and ripped out the photographs and wrote poems to fit the images of Steiglitz, Karsh, and other American photographers.

I wrote dinosaur stories. One, caused by *The Lost World,* rose from the sea late at night and fell in love with a lighthouse and the cry of the foghorn. The foghorn itself was a super metaphor of all the melancholy funerals and sad remembrances in history. That story, with its haunted dinosaur and foghorn, I sent to John Huston, who then hired me to write the screenplay of *Moby-Dick,* a book swarming with immense images—metaphors—from the nineteenth century.

So it was that the film beasts first encountered when I was five changed my life at thirty-three, and changed it forever.

I remember going to the dime store when I was ten, buying packets of film clips which, held up to the sun, were snippets from motion pictures released during my childhood. Thus, without knowing it, I lifted metaphors from the past into the light.

Along the way a wild hunger seized me for more films. In my teens I saw as many as five or six motion pictures a week. Often not able to afford them, I sneaked in or got to know the theater manager and convinced him to seat me for the price of a newspaper.

Walking through the Academy of Motion Picture Arts and Sciences some years ago I gazed at its huge wall posters, eighty of them, from the greatest pictures of all time. I had seen every one, so mad was my hunger for what happened in the dark theater with the giant shapes of light.

Things to Come, released in theaters when I was sixteen, showed Cabell and Passworthy watching their children shot off to the moon from a giant space gun. As the film ends, Cabell speaks the metaphor that changed my life further: "Which shall it be, all of space, eternity, and immortality, or the grave? Choose. The stars or the dust." I staggered from the theater, crushed with this revelation, to continue writing times as not yet born.

In those years, too, I attended the Chicago World's Fair to find myself surrounded by the colors, shapes, and concepts of the future and all the ideas coming to birth. So wild was my enthusiasm that my parents had to drag me out of the grounds at midnight; I wanted to stay and live with all those promises and never go home. From then on I dreamed of some day helping to create another Fair.

I did just that when I was offered a chance to blueprint and script the entire upper floor of the United States Pavilion at the New York World's Fair in 1964. I moved on from that to lock in the interior images for Spaceship Earth at Disney's Epcot Center.

So, as you can see, my life has been nothing but a movement—a dance—among all these images. My problem is fearing to use the "metaphor" word too often, but I cannot escape it when I look at all of my poems, stories, and plays. People remember them because the images loom so large that once seen or read, they are hard to forget.

My love of outsize concepts often causes trouble. Many years ago I took Fritz Lang, the famed German film director, to a screening of *Fahrenheit 451.* The film ends with the Book People wandering in a gentle downfall of snow, reciting lines from the books that they love. This terrific scene, with the music of Bernard Hermann, ends the film on a wonderful note.

On the way home Fritz kept shouting, "Goddamn it to hell! I hate those stupid people wandering in the wilderness, talking their books!"

"Fritz," I cried, "it's not supposed to be real! It's what we hope could happen, but never will."

"Goddamn it to hell!" said Fritz.

On the other hand, Sam Peckinpah came to me wanting to film one of my novels.

"How will you do it?" I asked.

"Rip the pages out of your book," said Sam, "and stuff them in the camera."

He was right.

Because I am, in essence, a nineteenth century writer. Consider the works of Nathaniel Hawthorne, Melville, Edgar Allen Poe, or Mark Twain. Not since their time have there been many writers who illustrate their concepts with such unforgettable images. I'm lucky to have been raised on these writers.

As the Paris newspaper *Le Monde* said in a recent article, I am a collector of metaphors and I did it all without knowing what I was doing.

One final metaphor. When my friend Patrick Kachurka asked what I wanted for Christmas, I replied, "A Flexible Flyer."

"A what?" he said.

"A Flexible Flyer," I said. "When I was a kid we could only afford a sled you controlled with your feet. The rich kids owned Flexible Flyers with steering gear up front. So, finally, I would love to own a Flexible Flyer."

Now my Flexible Flyer stands on my library hearth, next to the spade George Bernard Shaw used to plant a tree in London on his seventieth birthday, next to a golden statue of the goddess Sette, who guarded the tomb of Tutankhamen. Will I paint "Rosebud" on the sled? I just might.

Here are my creatures, my visions, my symbols, my *metaphors,* displayed by Jerry Weist. Here is the lonely beast in love with the lighthouse and the melancholy foghorn. Here is the Tyrannosaus Samurai-Warrior striding through a lost jungle. Here are my wondrous butterflies, waiting to stepped on, to change history.

I leave Jerry Weist's history of my images for you to turn, page by page, one by one. I hope your reaction to this will not be Fritz's "Goddamn it," but instead dear Sam's response, "Rip the pages out and stuff them in the camera."

—Los Angeles, California
January 2002

BRADBURY

An Illustrated Life

Photographs by Kaufmann & Fabry, Co., of the 1934 World's Fair: A Century of Progress, from two different *Official Pictures* books. (© The Reuben H. Donnelley Corporations, 1933/A Century of Progress, Chicago, 1934)

Early Life, Early Fandom

Photograph © Glynn Crain, 2001

The Chicago 1934 World's Fair. As a young boy, Ray went to the 1,000,000 B.C. exhibit, which featured some of the first automatically animated dinosaurs—viewed by means of a moving circular pathway. The young Bradbury decided to walk backward on this moving pathway to extend the clearly too brief allotted viewing time for as long as possible. He recalls that eventually, "they had to ask me to leave." Despite this unwanted ejection, the Chicago World's Fair left impressions on the boy that would last a lifetime.

Bradbury's second home, in Tucson, Arizona. (Photograph courtesy of the collection of Ray Bradbury)

Young Bradbury selling newspapers in California, 1930s. Ray made enough money selling newspapers during the 1930s to fuel his purchase of science fiction pulp magazines, continue his exploration of film, and eventually publish his own fanzine. (Photograph courtesy of the collection of Donn Albright)

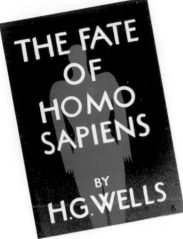

Covers from books by H. G. Wells: TOP LEFT: *The Fate of Homo Sapiens,* TOP CENTER: *The Time Machine,* TOP RIGHT: *The Shape of Things to Come,* ABOVE LEFT: *The Invisible Man,* ABOVE RIGHT: *Things to Come* (English movie edition). ABOVE CENTER: Illustrations from *Once Upon a Time,* the book of fairy tales given to Bradbury by his aunt Neva at Christmas 1925. Also pictured are the cover and title page from *Once Upon a Time.* The work of H. G. Wells, like that of Jules Verne, would exert a tremendous influence on the young Bradbury. (© Secker & Warburg/Hutchinson/Collins & Sons/Cresset Press/Readers Library/Rand McNally Co., 1924–45)

LEFT: *The Magic of Oz,* by L. Frank Baum, illustrated by John R. Neill. Bradbury's young imagination was fired by the tales of Oz and its characters. (*The Magic of Oz* © 1919, The Reilly & Lee Company, Chicago)

LEFT: The inside cover of Ray Bradbury's copy of *Once Upon a Time.* The inscription from his aunt Neva is clear in the upper left circle: "TO SHORTY BRADBURY, FROM NEVA BRADBURY, DEC. 25, 1925." Throughout his entire career Bradbury has expressed his gratitude toward his aunt Neva, who first helped spark the boy's imagination by reading to him. This very special book of fairy tales has been held sacred by Bradbury since it was given to him when he was five years old. (Photograph courtesy of the collection of Ray Bradbury. *Once Upon a Time* © 1925, Rand McNally Co.)

ABOVE: Ray Bradbury holding the American first edition of *From the Earth to the Moon*, by Jules Verne. (Photograph © Glynn Crain 2001)

BELOW LEFT: Cover for *Twenty Thousand Leagues Under the Seas*, the first edition, 1873.

BELOW RIGHT: Interior illustration by Hildibrand in *Journal d'Education et de Récréation*, edited by J. Hetzel, 1871. (© Geo. M. Smith & Co. 1871, Bibliothéque d'Education et de Récréation, 1871)

Bradbury muses now that "walking backward" is the perfect metaphor for his life, as through his work he has "walked backward" to reach the future of tomorrow.

Ray Bradbury was born August 22, 1920, in Waukegan Illinois. His early childhood was happy, and greatly enriched by loving family members who exposed the young boy to a wide variety of the surrounding culture. Ultimately, "Shorty," as his family called him, would forge an almost universal interest in the world that surrounded him.

By the time Bradbury was three years old he had seen Lon Chaney in *The Hunchback of Notre Dame*. His beloved aunt Neva often read to him from a book of fairy tales that she gave to him for Christmas in 1925. Within the next few years he would experience his first Oz books, see another important Lon Chaney film, *The Phantom of the Opera*, and be introduced to the pulp science fiction magazines through the fall 1928 issue of *Amazing Stories Quarterly*. It was a short jump from these experiences to the romance of Edgar Rice Burroughs's Mars novels, the visually rich world of *Tarzan of the Apes* comic strips

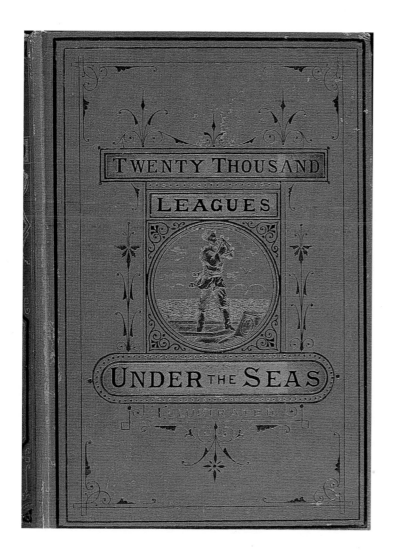

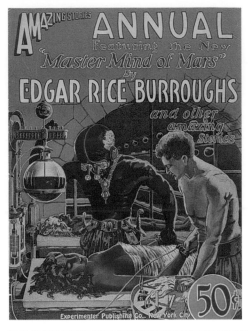

ABOVE: *Amazing Stories Annual,* vol. 1, no. 1, 1928; cover and interior illustration by Frank R. Paul. This pulp magazine featured an entire novel and carried one of Paul's most renowned covers. *Amazing Stories,* February 1927; cover artwork by Frank R. Paul illustrating a scene from Edgar Rice Burroughs's *The Land That Time Forgot.* Bradbury, like other young science fiction fans who would later become authors (including Isaac Asimov, Frederik Pohl, and Arthur C. Clarke) was drawn to the pulp magazines by the magic and power of Frank R. Paul's cover artwork. (© Hugo Gernsback Publications, 1927–28)

ABOVE: J. Allen St. John, interior illustrations from *Thuvia, Maid of Mars.* Page 220: "A steel blade pierced the very center of his heart . . ." Front plate: "As the great thoat and his rider hurtled past, Carthoris swung his long-sword in a mighty cut." This was the fourth Mars novel by Edgar Rice Burroughs, published in 1920, the year Bradbury was born. (© Edgar Rice Burroughs, Inc., 1920)

in the Sunday newspapers, and, eventually, the magic of *Buck Rogers,* illustrated by Dick Calkins. The worlds of the circus, magic, Blackstone the Magician, and Jules Verne novels also enthralled the young Bradbury.

Bradbury the author has remained devoted to these passions of his childhood. This simple truth is evident throughout the chapters of this book, and gave America an author who would develop working relationships with almost every aspect of popular culture in this country. It was—and continues to be— a remarkable journey, and as these chapters unfold the reader will witness time and again how the "sense of wonder" of Bradbury's youth has remained the wellspring for his imagination throughout his entire career.

The Edgar Rice Burroughs Effect. Bradbury's love for the work of Edgar Rice Burroughs came straight from the heart. His uncle Bion's home held a great number of the early Burroughs books, and the Mars series captivated Bradbury. Both J. Allen St. John and Frank R. Paul would further spark Bradbury's imagination with their illustrations for Burroughs's novels, and by the fall of 1932 he had begun a very special scrapbook, cutting and pasting *Tarzan of the Apes,* illustrated by Harold Foster, from the Sunday newspapers. For

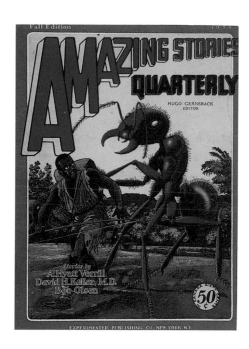

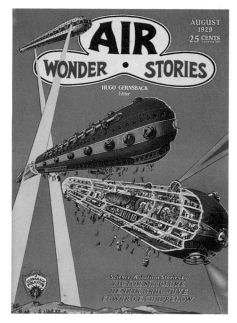

ABOVE LEFT: The very first science fiction magazine seen by Bradbury, the fall 1928 issue of *Amazing Stories Quarterly*.

ABOVE CENTER: Back cover painting by Frank R. Paul, titled *Taurus—Pleiades and Aldebaran* for *Amazing Stories*.

ABOVE RIGHT, AND RIGHT: Frank R. Paul covers for *Air Wonder Stories* November 1929, and *Wonder Stories Quarterly* for spring 1931. (© Ziff Davis & Co. and Hugo Gernsback Publications, 1928, 1929, 1931, and 1939)

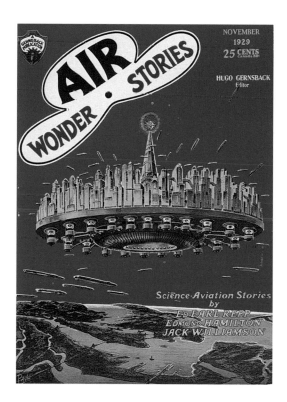

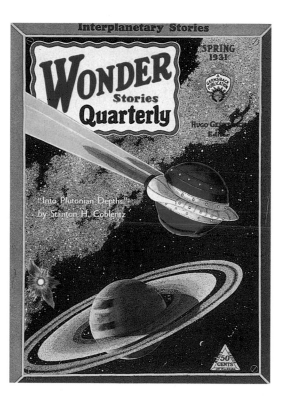

Christmas of 1932 Bradbury was given his first toy-dial typewriter, resulting in a full-blown sequel to *John Carter of Mars*. Bradbury's early love for the romance and fiction of Mars was already evolving from the planet envisioned by Percival Lowell and Edgar Rice Burroughs, and would blossom as he began his first short stories for the pulp magazines nearly fifteen years later.

Lon Chaney as Quasimodo in *The Hunchback of Notre Dame,* 1923. (© Universal Pictures, 1923)

Interior illustration by Harry Clarke, *The Dagger Dropped Gleaming Upon the Sable Carpet,* for *The Pit and the Pendulum,* by Edgar Allan Poe, in *Tales of Mystery and Imagination,* 1933. (© Tudor Publishing Co., 1933)

The Horror Movie Effect. As happened to the title character in the movie version of H. G. Wells's *The Invisible Man,* Ray Bradbury's mind "lit up" when he first was taken to the movie theater to see Lon Chaney in *The Hunchback of Notre Dame.* Although he was just three years old, Bradbury immediately fell in love with the dark theater and its wonders. He has many times since declared that his "life was changed forever" by watching the performance of Lon Chaney as Quasimodo. It was at this time, too, that his aunt Neva exposed him to Edgar Allan Poe, reading to the boy from *Tales of Mystery and Imagination.* Whereas most people would be swept away by the horror elements inherent in Poe and Quasimodo, Bradbury instead found the seeds for metaphor. He would use this tool for comparison and likeness almost immediately when he began to write.

Early science fiction "monster" fans Ray Bradbury (left, holding skull and knife) and his friend Forrest J Ackerman, in Los Angeles, 1938 or 1939. Ray Harryhausen made the mask for Bradbury, and later that day the young monsters attended the Paramount Theatre to see *Cat and the Canary,* where the young Bradbury "scared a girl in the audience" with his monster mask! (© Photograph courtesy of the collection of Forrest J Ackerman)

Lon Chaney unmasked in *The Phantom of the Opera,* 1925. (© Universal Films, 1925)

LEFT: Lon Chaney masked in *The Phantom of the Opera,* 1925. (© Universal Films, 1925)

RIGHT: One-sheet poster for *The Phantom of the Opera,* 1925. There were eight one-sheet posters for this famous film. This version is best remembered for showing The Phantom in full figure. (© Universal Films, 1925)

Oil-on-canvas painting by Frank R. Paul, for the cover of *Science Fiction Quarterly* no. 2, winter 1941. Paul's cover artwork would dominate the Hugo Gernsback magazine titles throughout the 1930s and exert a profound impact on young Ray Bradbury. This early interest in science-fiction artists later manifested itself in the maturing author's own drawings and cartoons for some of his early book cover designs. Bradbury would eventually develop close working relationships with artists such as Joseph Mugnaini, Hannes Bok, and the stable of artists at EC. (© Hugo Gernsback Publications/Frank R. Paul estate, 1941)

WHAT WILL THE NEXT HUNDRED YEARS BRING TO MANKIND?

H.G. WELLS' "THINGS TO COME"

An **ALEXANDER KORDA** *production*

with **RAYMOND MASSEY   RALPH RICHARDSON
SIR CEDRIC HARDWICKE   PEARL ARGYLE
MARGARETTA SCOTT** *and a cast of* **20,000**
Directed by **WILLIAM CAMERON MENZIES**
A London Film ~ Released thru United Artists

ABOVE: Poster for six-sheet to the movie *Things to Come* written by H. G. Wells, 1936. (© London Films, 1936)

RIGHT: The author H. G. Wells on the set of *Things to Come*, in 1936. Wells maintained that all he wanted was to "entertain." However, he negotiated nearly complete control over the working script and production for this movie. (© London Films, 1936)

ABOVE: Original art for a *Tarzan* Sunday strip by Burne Hogarth, circa 1940s. This original was hand-colored by the artist for Danton Burroughs in 1993. (© United Feature Syndicate, ERB Inc., 1940)

LEFT: Original hand-watercolored *Prince Valiant* strip by Hal Foster, Sunday page dated 8/7/38, no. 78 in this series. This is the only page confirmed as hand-colored by Hal Foster. Bradbury discovered Foster through his brilliant and exciting work for the *Tarzan of the Apes* Sunday pages, and became a dedicated collector of *Prince Valiant*. As late as 1953 science fiction fans could find small ads placed by Bradbury in the *Fantasy Advertiser* in a quest to locate specific *Prince Valiant* pages to fill out his collection. (© King Features Syndicate, 1938)

Bradbury Likes Funnies. At a very early age Bradbury began to cut out and save daily and Sunday comic strips. In 1929 he discovered *Buck Rogers* in his local paper, and shortly thereafter began his collection of *Tarzan of the Apes* and *Flash Gordon.* His love for the comics was organic, and to this day he remains enthusiastic about this art form. During the 1950s, as his writing career was about to reach a

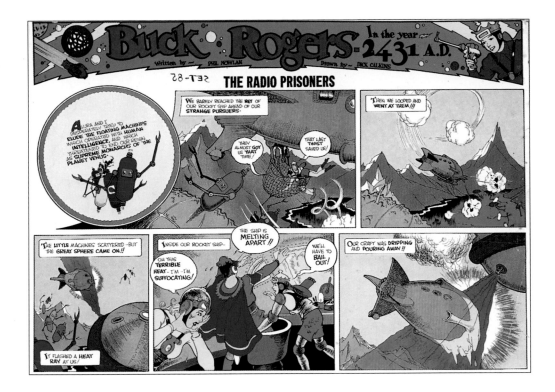

Buck Rogers partial proof Sunday page from 1931. (© The John F. Dille Co., 1931)

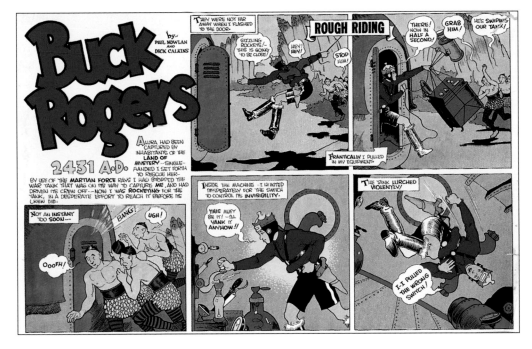

Buck Rogers partial proof Sunday page from 1931. The *Buck Rogers* Sundays were credited to Lt. Dick Calkins, but were in fact drawn by Russell Keaton. Keaton also drew *Sky Roads* before his own strip, *Flying Jenny,* was launched in 1939. His promising career was cut short at its peak when he died in early 1945, at the age of thirty-four during war-related training exercises. (© The John F. Dille Co., 1931)

new level of sophistication (it was at this time that he embarked on writing the script for John Huston's film *Moby Dick*), he bravely defended his early passion, and his stories were adapted for EC Comics by Al Feldstein.

"In the earliest years of the LASFS, Ray came to downtown L.A. to Clifton's cafeteria for the semiweekly 'scientifiction' meetings, sometimes I suspect

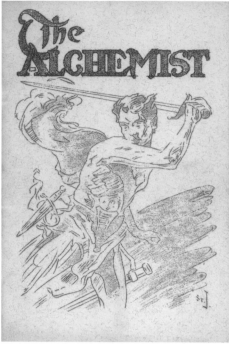

ABOVE LEFT: *New Worlds,* vol. 1, no. 4 (Aug. 1939), a British fanzine. Cover by Harry Turner. Editor: Ted Carnell, assistant: Arthur C. Clarke. This issue contains a humorous piece by Bradbury, "Mathematica Minus," which was (according to an accompanying note) reprinted from the July 1938 *Imagination!* fanzine. It ends with this poem: *I think that I shall never see / A science-fiction fan like me,/ Who sits and dreams of rocket ships / And nourish-tablets upon my lips. / I read my magazines all day / With age they're brown, and I am gray. / I'd go to Mars myself, know well, / If it weren't for this darned padded cell.* (© The Science Fiction Association, 1939)

ABOVE CENTER: *The Alchemist,* vol. 1, no. 5 (Feb. 1941). Cover art by J. Allen St. John. In what is the second-to-last issue of this Denver, Colorado, fanzine appears a humorous piece by Bradbury titled "I Am Positively Not Robert Bloch!" (© *The Alchemist,* 1941)

ABOVE RIGHT: *The Damn Thing,* vol. 1, no. 2 (Dec. 1940). Cover art by Ray Bradbury. "Dictator": T. Bruce Yerke. This Los Angeles fanzine contains a story by Bradbury, "Genie Trouble!" (© T. B. Yerke, LASFL, 1940)

LEFT: *Fantasy Magazine,* vol. 4, no. 6, Scientifilm issue (May 1935), edited by Julius Schwartz. Schwartz would later become Bradbury's first agent in the science fiction market. (© Julius Schwartz, *Fantasy Magazine,* 1935)

because the limeade and lime Jell-O were free and he was pretty penniless. He was loud, boisterous, always hamming it up with impersonations of W. C. Fields or Hitler (I don't remember Jolson, although, like me, he was a great Jolie fan); perhaps *obstreperous* was the word for Ray in those days.

ABOVE LEFT: *Imagination!,* vol. 1, no. 8 (May 1938). "Organ of the Los Angeles Chapter, SCIENCE FICTION LEAGUE." Cover by Hannes Bok. "Verse of the Imagi-nation!" by Farsaci, Bradbury, and Morojo. (© LASFL, 1938)

ABOVE CENTER: *Imagination!,* vol. 1, no. 9 (June 1938). Cover artwork by Bradbury. Contains "How to Become a Sci-Fic Fan [sic]," by Bradbury, and an amusing bio of Bradbury (which lists his favorite authors, etc.). (© LASFL, 1938)

ABOVE RIGHT: *Imagination!,* vol. 1, no. 10 (July 1938). Contains "Mathematica Minus," by Bradbury. (© LASFL, 1938)

RIGHT: *Imagination!,* vol. 1, no. 6 (March 1938). Cover by Bradbury, perhaps his finest early science fiction fanzine effort. (© LASFL, 1938)

I've often philosophized how lucky that we didn't strangle him and rob the world of one of the greatest literary talents and socially stimulating individuals of the twentieth century. A coruscating Roman candle in the pyrotechnical company of H. G. Wells, Aldous Huxley, Philip Wylie, Jacque Fresco, Hugo Gernsback, Arthur C. Clarke, Isaac Asimov, Robert Heinlein, and, yes Edgar Rice Burroughs, whom he loves. Keep on chronicling, O beloved Barsoomian in earthly disguise."

—Forrest J Ackerman,
Hollywood, Winter 2001

ABOVE LEFT: *Futuria Fantasia,* vol. 1, no. 1 (summer 1939). Cover by Hannes Bok. A fanzine edited by Bradbury. (Photograph courtesy of the collection of Donn Albright. © Ray Bradbury, 1939)

ABOVE RIGHT: *Futuria Fantasia,* vol. 1, no. 2 (fall 1939). Cover by Hannes Bok. Ray Bradbury did indeed crank the mimeograph machine himself during production on *Futuria Fantasia.* However, recent conversations with the author indicate that he had help with the stencil designs and stencil typewritten pages from other Los Angeles fans. (© Ray Bradbury, 1939)

LEFT: Young Bradbury, circa 1940–44, around the time he was working on *Futuria Fantasia.* (Photograph courtesy of the collection of Donn Albright. © Ray Bradbury)

The Fanzine *Imagination!* Ray Bradbury arrived in Los Angeles in 1934; he was thirteen years old. It was not until 1937 that he discovered the Los Angeles Science Fiction League, joined the club, and began friendships with Forrest J Ackerman, Henry Kuttner, Ray Harryhausen, Robert Heinlein, Hannes Bok, Jack Williamson, Edmond Hamilton, and a host of other science fiction authors and fans. During this time he contributed to numerous

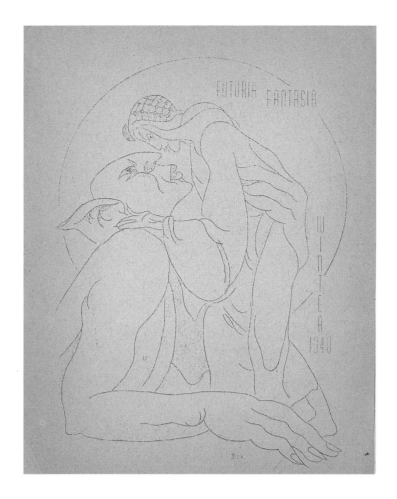

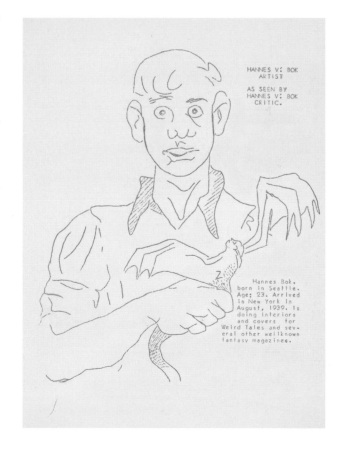

ABOVE LEFT: *Futuria Fantasia,* vol. 1, no. 3 (winter 1940). Cover by Hannes Bok. (Photograph courtesy of the collection of Donn Albright. © Ray Bradbury, 1940.)

ABOVE RIGHT: *Futuria Fantasia,* vol. 1, no. 4 (summer 1940). Cover by Hannes Bok. The final issue featured a photo-offset cover by Hannes Bok. (© Ray Bradbury, 1940)

RIGHT: "Hannes V. Bok, Artist, As Seen by Hannes V. Bok, Critic," for *Futuria Fantasia,* vol. 1, no. 4. The text reads: "Hannes Bok. Born in Seattle. Age: 23. Arrived in New York in August, 1939. Is doing interiors and covers for *Weird Tales* and several other well known fantasy magazines." (© Ray Bradbury, 1940)

fanzines, both as an artist and author. His association with Ackerman led to steady work for the fanzine *Imagination!,* and he would eventually mature into his own editor for *Futuria Fantasia.*

THE VERY EARLY RAY BRADBURY

Ray Bradbury was already a dedicated sci-fi fan when, in 1937, he discovered the Los Angeles Science Fantasy Society, which had been founded in 1935 as a chapter of Gernsback's Science Fiction League. Instantly, he became a super-active member and was there when the club initiated its official organ, *Imagination!*

Ray Bradbury with Bob Madle at the World Science Fiction Convention, 1939. Top row, left to right: V. Kidwell, Robert A. Madle, Earle Korshak, and Ray Bradbury. Bottom row, left to right: Mark Reinsberg, Jack Agnew, and Ross Rocklynne. From *FFF's Illustrated NYCon Review*. Producer: Julius Unger. Photographer: Joe Christoff. (© Fantasy Fiction Field, 1942)

THOUGHT AND SPACE
A Poem by Ray D. Bradbury (1940)

*Space—thy boundaries are
Time and time alone.
No earth-born rocket,
seedling skyward sown,
Will ever reach your cold,
infinite end,
This power is not Man's to
build or send.
Great deities laugh down,
venting their mirth,
At struffling bipeds on
a cloud-wrapped Earth,
Chained solid on a war-swept,
waning globe,
For FATE, who witnesses,
to pry and probe.*

*BUT LIST! One weapon have
I stronger yet!
Prepare Infinity! And
Gods regret!
Thought, quick as light,
shall pierce the veil,
To reach the lost be-
ginnings Holy Grail.
Across the sullen void on
soundless trail,
Where new-spawned suns and
chilling planets wail,
One thought shall travel
'midst the gods' playthings,
Past cindered globes where
choking flame still sings.*

*No wall of force yet have ye
firmly wrought,
That chains the supreme
strength of purest thought.
Unleashed, without a body's
slacking hold,
Thought leaves the ancient
Earth behind to mold.
And when galaxies have
heeded DEATH,
And welcomed lastly SPACE'S
poisoned breath,
Still shall thought travel
as an arrow flown.
SPACE—thy boundaries are
TIME—AND TIME ALONE!*

Imagination! started as a hektographed publication, but soon changed to the mimeograph, which enabled more copies to be printed. Ray was noted for being young, noisy, nosey, and into all aspects of the club and its new publication. He wrote short, snappy, humorous—sometimes ghastly—articles. A good example is the one titled "Why Ghouls Leave Home," which appeared in the July 1939 issue of my fan magazine *Fantascience Digest*. It was about his pet ghoul, Moses Gable, whose favorite dinner song is "I can have archaic and eat it too!" Ray said Moses was playing with matches and was afraid "He would make an ash of himself." I should mention that because of Ray's appearance in this issue of *FD*, it is now worth about $150! Such is fame!

During Ray's early years in the LASFS, he became friendly with Forrest J Ackerman, who, among many other things, was *Imagination!*'s editor. When 1939 rolled around and it was time to attend the first world sf convention, NYCon, Ray joined Forry and his lady friend Morojo (Myrtle R. Douglas) to comprise the trio who made the trek across country to partake of the wonders of the first WorldCon.

NYCon was a marvelous experience. About two hundred fans and authors attended, most of whom knew each other through correspondence or fan activities, but were meeting for the first time. Forry and Morojo made a handsome couple dressed in costumes inspired by the movie *Things to Come*. (This was really the beginning of costumes and the masquerade at conventions. At the next convention, CHICon [1940], the costume ball was part of the program.)

The third day of NYCon featured a softball game between the Queens Science Fiction League and the Philadelphia S-F Society. It was a sloppily played game, the most important thing about it being the fact that Ray and Charles D. Hornig (famous sf editor of *Wonder Stories, Science Fiction,* and *Future Fiction*) were scorekeepers. The final score was 23–11 (Queens over Philadelphia), so the scorekeepers were busier than the players.

From left to right: Edmond Hamilton's sister, Ray Bradbury, Edmond Hamilton, and Leigh Bracket, circa 1946–47. This photograph was taken just after the LASFS period of fan activity. (Photograph courtesy of the collection of Ray Bradbury)

After the game, someone came up with the suggestion that we go to Coney Island and have fun. I don't remember all who went, but the group I *do* recall consisted of Ross Rocklynne (famous author) and fans Earle Korshak, Mark Reinsberg, Vincent Kitwell, Jack Agnew, and your humble scribe. We arranged to meet others there, including Julius Schwartz.

Before getting on the subway to Coney Island (or was it the elevated?), we stopped at a small restaurant. Everyone was on a tight budget, so when the waiters took our orders, we ordered either a hamburger or a bowl of soup. All except Ray, who said, "Just bring me a bowl of hot water." When the food arrived, Ray took the ketchup bottle and poured some into the hot water, making a bowl of delicious tomato soup! So much for limited budgets.

It was July 4 when we arrived at Coney Island—as it was when we started. It was a grand evening—we rode the roller coasters, ate ice cream, tossed firecrackers (Agnew was nabbed by a cop as he tossed one—but the cop was understanding). Someone said, "Let's have a picture made," so we did—in an old tin lizzie. The

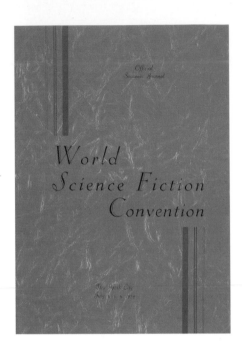

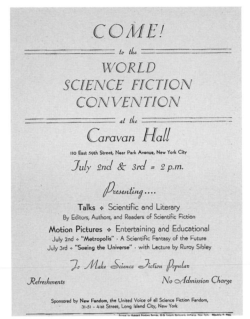

seven of us who started the trip together are in the photo. At the time we could not have realized how important this photo would become—primarily because Ray is in it. It should be mentioned that, many years later, Julius Schwartz published an article in one of his DC comic magazines called "The Greatest Night of My Life." The article detailed July 4 at Coney Island—it was written by Ray Bradbury.

Those of us still remaining will always remember that evening at Coney Island. It was, indeed, the climax of the first WorldCon. I'm sure Ray remembers the evening most of all, as the following two anecdotes will attest.

Bruce Francis was an sf fan—but primarily a Bradbury fan. He visited Ray one time and, during dinner, mentioned he was working with me. His wife said to Ray, "Bob Madle—isn't he in the picture?" Ray nodded and took Bruce to his basement where, on the wall, was a blown-up copy of the Coney Island photo.

When Ray was guest of honor at the Atlanta World SF Convention—about fifteen years ago—we both met at a party. We hadn't seen each other for decades, but Ray looked at me and exclaimed "New York, Coney Island, 1939!"

It was great to have been with Ray on the greatest night of his life.

—Robert A. Madle, 2001

RAY BRADBURY AT NYCON/ FIRST WORLDCON

"So this rambunctious ambitious kid was keen to attend the first World Science Fiction Convention in New York on the Fourth of July, 1939, but his only transportation at that time was a pair of roller skates and he doubted they'd get him to Gotham. I hated to see a grown boy cry and I was a bachelor at the time living rent free with my maternal grandparents and making a munificent eighty-five cents an hour working at the Academy of Motion Picture Arts and Sciences, so I volunteered to lend the money to Ray to spend three and a half days and nights on a Greyhound bus. My memory is that it was fifty dollars I lent him, but every time I'm in the audience when he tells the tale of the loan for a friend it grows; at last recording it was up to ninety five dollars. Maybe he takes inflation into account. It took him a couple of years but he faithfully repaid me. Fifty bucks may not seem like much now, but sixty years ago, out of the 185 of us at the Con, only twenty-eight could afford the banquet and I couldn't afford to lend the money to Ray. After all, it was a dollar a plate. No food, you understand, just a plate. And on top of that you were expected to be generous and (*oy gevalt*) leave a TEN-CENT TIP!"

—Forrest J Ackerman, 2001

TOP: Forrest J Ackerman at the first WorldCon, in futuristic costume speaking before the attending fans, 1939. This photograph was taken by attending member Jack Darrow. (Photograph courtesy of the collection of Doug Ellis, used with permission. © Jack Darrow, 1939.)

ABOVE: From *FFF's Illustrated NYCon Review*. Left to right: Mark Reinsburg, Louis Kuslan, Jack Agnew, John V. Baltadonis, unidentified, Walter Sullivan, Ray Bradbury, and Forrest J Ackerman. Upon viewing this photograph, Ray remarked that he was doing what he loved most at the time: talking to other fans about science fiction. (© NYCon, 1939)

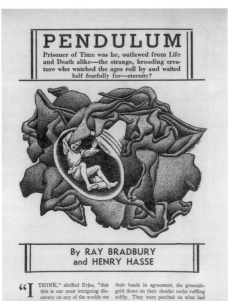

2

From Pulps to Slicks

Photograph © Glynn Crain, 2001

A child of the Depression, Ray Bradbury grew up knowing he wanted to become a writer. His first published efforts appeared during the 1930s in science fiction "fanzines," and from there it was perhaps inevitable that he would eventually see his first stories published in the pulp magazines of the period. During his younger years, Bradbury sought out help, advice, and criticism from older, established writers such as Robert Heinlein, Henry Kuttner, Leigh Brackett, Henry Hasse (with whom he would briefly collaborate on his first published work), and Jack Williamson. All of these authors had valuable experience within the pulp world—of its many pitfalls and too few advantages.

Weird Tales gladly accepted Bradbury's early horror stories, unique as they were, and he enjoyed early recognition and popularity. However, as his stories began to be published in science fiction pulp magazines such as *Planet Stories, Astounding Science-Fiction* (editor John Campbell *did* accept three Bradbury short-short stories!), *Thrilling Wonder Stories,* and *Super Science Stories,* a strange thing began to happen: The sf pulp editors began to reject Bradbury stories. Although these editors had spent the past decade calling for "fresh," "new," and "original" material (the call being echoed by fans and readers in fanzines and on letters-to-the-editor pages), early reaction to Bradbury's work

Hannes Bok, title illustration for "Subterfuge," from *Astonishing Stories,* April 1943. It was fitting that many of Bradbury's early pulp stories were illustrated by his close friend and associate Hannes Bok. Bradbury was responsible for introducing Bok's work to the publishers of *Weird Tales* in 1939, and they immediately hired him. Bok quickly placed illustrations with many other science fiction magazines following his debut in *Weird Tales.* (© Fictioneers, Inc. [Popular], 1943)

ABOVE LEFT: Humiston, title illustration for "The Crowd," from *Weird Tales,* May 1943. (© *Weird Tales,* 1943)

ABOVE CENTER: Lawrence Stern Stevens, double-page illustration for "King of the Grey Spaces," from the December 1943 issue of *Famous Fantastic Mysteries.* Stevens was right behind Virgil Finlay in fan popularity, and this illustration was one of his more successful efforts for a Bradbury story. (© All-Fiction Field, Inc. [Popular], 1943)

ABOVE RIGHT: Mark Marchioni, title illustration for "Promotion to Satellite," from *Thrilling Wonder Stories,* fall 1943. (© Standard Magazines, Inc., 1943)

CENTER LEFT: Joe Doolin, title illustration for "Morgue Ship," from the summer 1944 issue of *Planet Stories.* (© Love Romances Publishing Co., Inc./Fiction House, 1944)

CENTER RIGHT: Jeffrey Knight Potter, title illustration for "Lazarus Come Forth," from *Planet Stories,* winter 1944. (© Love Romances Publishing Co., Inc./Fiction House, 1944)

LEFT: Hannes Bok, original artwork for title illustration of "The Silence," printed in *Super Science Stories,* January 1949. This color illustration reinforces a timeless truth for the best of the pulp illustrators: they were bound to lose 10 to 30 percent of the detail of any given black-and-white illustration once it was reproduced on the low-quality pulp paper from which the magazines got their popular name. (© Fictioneers, Inc. [Popular], 1949)

criticized it for not toeing the "party line" of what a science fiction story should be.

Although this briefly sent Bradbury into the pages of the detective pulps, he soon returned to the science fiction magazines. He would forge for himself (and, eventually, a new generation of younger writers), a space within the

ABOVE LEFT: Mayan, title illustration for "Touch and Go!," from the November 1948 issue of *Detective Book Magazine*. (© Fiction House, Inc., 1948)

ABOVE, CENTER LEFT: Artist unknown, title illustration for "Hell's Half-Hour," from the March 1945 issue of *New Detective Magazine*. (© Fictioneers, Inc. [Popular], 1945)

ABOVE, CENTER RIGHT: Artist unknown, title illustration for "Corpse-Carnival," from the July 1945 issue of *Dime Mystery Magazine*. (© Popular Publications, Inc., 1945)

ABOVE RIGHT: Artist unknown, title illustration for "A Careful Man Dies," from the November 1946 issue of *New Detective Magazine*. (© Fictioneers, Inc. [Popular], 1946)

field where he could write stories that included new ideas (central to science fiction), a more literate writing style (sorely missing from most of these magazines), and a totally new use of poetic vision and metaphor (as yet almost unexplored by authors of the day). In a field known for reaching beyond accepted boundaries, Bradbury challenged the science fiction editors and readers of the 1940s to expand their horizons even further.

The editors and readers took him up on the challenge, and Bradbury grew to be one of the most popular pulp authors in the genre. It was at this point that he did something that few science fiction authors have been able to do—he leapt from the "genre" world of the pulps to the "mainstream" milieu of the slick magazines.

This chapter provides a chronological overview of the rich progression of illustration that accompanied these

ABOVE: Hannes Bok, original artwork for title illustration for "I, Mars," printed in *Super Science Stories*, April 1949. (© Fictioneers, Inc. [Popular], 1949)

early published stories. It is remarkable to note the range of excellent artists commissioned for Bradbury stories—from his very beginnings in *Weird Tales* to the later, more colorful and sophisticated work found in *Esquire* and *The Saturday Evening Post*. Never before in American letters had an author of such humble beginnings broken through in such a fashion. As history has shown, the young Bradbury was only beginning to flex his literary muscles, as he expanded his use of metaphor and embraced American popular culture.

15¢

NOV.

DIME MYSTERY MAGAZINE

COMBINED WITH 10 STORY MYSTERY

THE SMALL ASSASSIN
STARTLING NOVELETTE
by RAY BRADBURY

BLASSINGAME
KEENE
PLUNKETT
AND OTHERS

THE TOWER OF STINGING DEATH
SPINE-TINGLING NOVEL OF HIDDEN MENACE
by R. SPRAGUE HALL

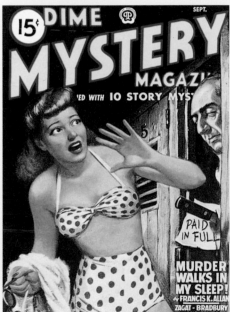

OVERLEAF: Peter Stevens, cover painting for November 1946 issue of *Dime Mystery Magazine*. This was the only pulp cover for a detective title on which a Bradbury story was featured. (© Popular Publications, Inc., 1946)

TOP, FAR LEFT: *Dime Mystery Magazine,* 1945. (© Popular Publications, Inc., 1945)

TOP, LEFT: Raphael De Soto, cover painting for the July 1945 issue of *Dime Mystery Magazine*. This issue featured two Bradbury stories, "Dead Men Rise Up Never" and "Corpse-Carnival" (as D. R. Banat). (© Popular Publications, Inc., 1945)

CENTER, FAR LEFT: Peter Stevens, cover painting for the January 1948 issue of *Dime Mystery Magazine*. This issue featured the Bradbury story "The Candy Skull." (© Popular Publications, Inc., 1948)

CENTER, LEFT: Raphael De Soto, cover painting for the September 1947 issue of *Dime Mystery Magazine*. This issue featured "Wake for the Dead," which was later retitled "The Coffin" and included in Bradbury's first book, *Dark Carnival*, published by August Derleth's press Arkham House. (© Popular Publications, Inc., 1947)

BOTTOM, LEFT: Ray Bradbury circa the early 1940s. The back of this photograph is signed "Hello! Hannes! This is Bradbury!" This photo is rare in its depiction of Bradbury with an automobile; he is quite vocal about his extreme dislike of cars. As a young child, Bradbury witnessed a tragic automobile accident, the memory of which resulted in nightmares that persisted well into his adult years. The experience inspired one short story, "The Crowd," and discouraged Bradbury from ever learning to drive. (© The Hannes Bok Estate)

Ray Bradbury and *Weird Tales.* Ray Bradbury was given a special place within the pages of *Weird Tales* from the beginning of his association with the magazine. His very first published *Weird Tales* story, "The Candle," was published in the November 1942 issue. Unlike other magazines, whose editors tried to impose their own writing prejudices on authors, *Weird Tales* accepted Bradbury's unique writing style, singular ideas, and content as they were. Many early Bradbury classics first appeared in *Weird Tales;* a handful were recently brought back to life in Bradbury's "novel" *From the Dust Returned.* Bradbury made another important connection through *Weird Tales:* Writer and publisher August Derleth recognized greatness in the young Bradbury, and committed himself to bringing into print the first collection of Bradbury's short stories. The result was the now famous, rare, and valuable hardcover book *Dark Carnival,* published by Derleth's company Arkham House.

The artists who illustrated Bradbury's *Weird Tales* stories were among the most famous of the time, including Ray's close friend the young artist Hannes Bok, whose work Bradbury introduced to the editors of *Weird Tales* at the 1939 World Science Fiction Convention.

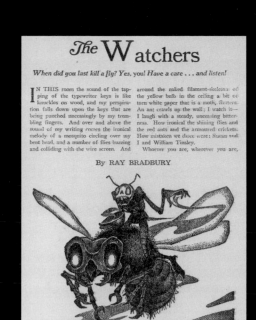

TOP: Boris Dolgov, title illustration for "There Was an Old Woman," from the July 1944 issue of *Weird Tales*. (© *Weird Tales*, 1944)

ABOVE: Boris Dolgov, title illustration for "The Night," from *Weird Tales*, July 1946. (© *Weird Tales*, 1946)

TOP: Boris Dolgov, title illustration for "The Watchers," from *Weird Tales*, May 1945. (© *Weird Tales*, 1945)

ABOVE: Lee Brown Coye, title illustration for "The Handler," from *Weird Tales*, January 1947. (© *Weird Tales*, 1947)

TOP: Boris Dolgov, title illustration for "The Traveller," from *Weird Tales*, March 1946. (© *Weird Tales*, 1946)

ABOVE: Lee Brown Coye, title illustration for "The October Game," from *Weird Tales*, March 1948. (© *Weird Tales*, 1948)

FAR LEFT: Hannes Bok, preliminary pencil sketch (no subject), circa 1950s. (© Hannes Bok estate, 2002)

RIGHT: Hannes Bok, original painting in gouache on board, untitled from the "mask" series, circa 1950s. (© Hannes Bok estate, 2002)

BELOW: Hannes Bok, circa 1940s, at the beginning of his career as a pulp illustrator. (Photo courtesy of the collection of Steve Kennedy. © Hannes Bok estate, 2002)

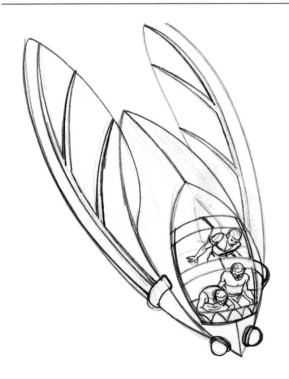

Ray Bradbury
670 Venice Blvd.,
Venice, California

October 26th, 1946

Dear Hannes:

You will think me a louse; nay, a footling drool!
I apologize for not having written the sooner. I
have been busy as hell, first, with traveling to
New Orleans, then with traveling to Arizona, then
with coming on to L.A., then with my girl-friend,
and lastly - with influenza. Sniffle.

It was good seeing you in New York a few weeks ago,
Hannes. I enjoyed visiting you ever so much. The
walk about town was invigorating, as was the food
at Gallagher's. I hope to see you again if I'm in
New York next April. I hope to have my novel finished
by then and bring it on to Simon and Schuster in
person. In the meantime, I wish you all the very
best in your dealings with editors during the long
chill winter. I would certainly like to see you
do some stylized child's books, and also some
unstylized free oils or water colors in a new
free mode. It might be refreshing and give you a
necessary hypo from time to time to give the free
sweeping splash a try. Listen to me: Sheldon Cheney
no less! Pay no mind. I'm quite ignorant.

I envy you, being in Manhattan in October. One of the
best months, I hear. The autumnal smell and the
autumnal wind. And the new shows opening.

Give my regards to Ron Clyne when you see him. Also
to any others I might know. And let me hear from
you after a decent interval, eh? I shall always
remember the night I left New York - after you so kindly
fetched my baggage for me hither and yon --- I watched
the tall neon-glow of the Empire State go on and on
over the horizon and sink down and down into night
blackness as my train moved slowly thirty miles on out
into the country toward Washington D.C. I tell you,
I had quite a lump in my throat for the old town.
Write soon, Hannes.

                              Your friend,

                              Ray

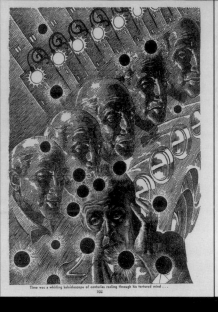

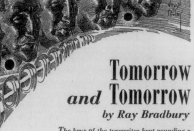

Tomorrow and Tomorrow
by Ray Bradbury

The keys of the typewriter kept pounding a message, and Steve Temple watched the words spell out—with no human hand on the machine.

UP TO the time he opened the door, the day hadn't been any different from all the other days. Walking Los Angeles hunting for a job he couldn't find, looking in store windows at food he couldn't buy, and wondering why the habit of living got so strong you couldn't break it even after you didn't want it any longer.

It hadn't been quite so bad as long as he had his typewriter to come home to. He could thumb his nose at the world outside for a while and build new ones—bright shiny worlds where he was a very glamorous guy indeed and never went hungry. He could kid himself, even, that some day he might be a writer, rolling in money and adoration.

He'd rather have parted with his right leg than his typewriter. But none of the Uncle Bennies were paying money for right legs, and a guy has to eat and pay his rent.

"Oh yeah?" he snarled at the door panel. "Name two reasons why?"

He couldn't name one. He unlocked it, closed it behind him, turned on the lights, and started to take off his hat.

He didn't. He forgot he had a hat, or a head under it. He just stood, staring.

There was a typewriter on the floor. It was his room, all right. Cracked ceiling, dingy paper, blue-striped pajamas trailing off an unmade wall bed, the memory of this morning's coffee.

It was not his typewriter.

There was no possible way for any typewriter to get there. That was bad enough, like finding a camel in the bath-

Time was a whirling kaleidoscope of centuries reeling through his tortured mind . . .

102 / 103

A Complete Novelet by **RAY BRADBURY**

Purple moved like blue vapor lights on the cobbled

avenues and odd animals scurried over the gray-red sand

....and the moon be still as bright

CHAPTER I
Voyagers From Earth

IT WAS so cold that when they first came from the ship into the night, Spender began to gather the dry Martian wood and build a small fire. He didn't say anything about a celebration, he merely gathered the wood, set fire to it and watched it burn.

In the flare that illumined the thin air of this dried up sea of Mars he looked over his shoulder and saw the rocket ship that had brought them all, Wilder and Cheroke, and Gibbs and McClure and himself across a silent black space of stars to land upon a dead, dreaming world.

Jeff Spender waited for the noise. He looked at the other men and waited for them to jump around and shout. It would happen as soon as the numbness of being the first men to Mars wore off.

Gibbs walked over to the freshly ignited fire and said, "Why don't we use the ship chemical fire instead of that wood?"

"Never mind," said Spender, not looking up.

It wouldn't be right, the first night on Mars, to make a loud noise, to introduce a strange silly bright thing like a stove. It would be a kind of imported blasphemy.

When Spender Stalks the Martian Hills, He Faces the Fate of an Idealist Gone Berserk!

78 / 79

The Million Year Picnic
By RAY BRADBURY

They were supposed to be starting on a picnic, a wonderful day of fun. But there was a gun in the boat, and too much food and equipment. . . . And just behind the veil of vacation—instead of the soft face of laughter—there was something hard and bony and terrifying.

Illustration by LEYDENFROST

SOMEHOW the idea was brought up by Mom that perhaps the whole family would enjoy a fishing trip. But they weren't Mom's words: Timothy knew that. They were Dad's words, and Mom used them for him, somehow.

Dad shuffled his feet in a cluster of Martian pebbles, and agreed. So immediately

PLANET STORIES
proudly presents one of the best science-fiction stories we have ever seen. Perhaps you will vote it the best!

ZERO HOUR
By RAY BRADBURY

40

Dwellers In Silence
By RAY BRADBURY

The fire grew in the sky.

A shattered Earth suddenly remembered poor Hathaway, marooned on Mars by the mad rush homeward, all alone. But—was he alone?

WHEN THE WIND CAME through the sky, he and his small family would sit in the stone hut and warm their hands over a small fire. The wind would stir the canal waters and almost blow the stars out of the sky, but Mr. Hathaway would sit contented and talk to his wife and his wife would talk back, and he would talk to his two daughters and his son about the old days on Earth, and they would all reply neatly.

It was the twentieth year after the Great War. Mars was a tomb planet. Whether or not Earth was the same was a matter for much silent debate for himself, or his family, on the long Martian nights. Then the dust storms came over the low hexagonal tomb buildings, whispering past the great ancient gargoyles on the iron mountains, blowing between the last standing pillars of an old city, and tearing away the plastic walls of a newer, American-built city that was nothing away into the sand, desolated.

51

"They are coming through the air and traveling along the ground," said Cecy, in her sleeping.

Lawrence S. Stevens, title illustration for "Homecoming," from *Famous Fantasic Mysteries,* December 1952. Without question one of the greatest pulp illustrations for any Ray Bradbury story, and a high-water mark for Lawrence Stern Stevens. This important story was printed in the Arkham House book *Dark Carnival.* (© Popular Publications, Inc., 19)

ABOVE: Virgil Finlay, double-page spread title illustration for "The Concrete Mixer," from *Thrilling Wonder Stories,* April 1949. (© Standard Magazines, Inc., 1949)

FAR LEFT: Astaria, title illustration for "The Naming of Names," from *Thrilling Wonder Stories,* August 1949. (© Standard Magazines, Inc., 1949)

LEFT: Mayan, title illustration for "Forever the Earth," from *Planet Stories,* spring 1950. (© Love Romances Publishing Co., Inc./Fiction House, 1950)

Kelly Freas, title illustration for "Lorelei of the Red Mist," from *Tops in Science Fiction,* fall 1953. (© Love Romances Publishing Co., Inc./Fiction House, 1953)

RIGHT: Kelly Freas, illustration for "Lorelei of the Red Mist," from *Tops in Science Fiction,* fall 1953. (© Love Romances Publishing Co., Inc./Fiction House, 1953)

OVERLEAF: Kelly Freas, original artwork for cover painting for "Lorelei of the Red Mist," printed in *Tops in Science Fiction,* fall 1953. Kelly Freas was the most beloved of all science fiction artists within science fiction fandom. His greatest work was done during the 1950s for John Campbell at *Astounding Science Fiction.* Part of his universal appeal was his ability to infuse original character into each illustration. With "Lorelei of the Red Mist," he breathed new life into an early pulp classic science fiction story that was being reprinted in *Tops in Science Fiction.* It would be his only illustration of a Ray Bradbury pulp story. (© Love Romances Publishing Co., Inc./Fiction House, 1953)

LORELEI OF THE RED MIST

body had lain before the life went out of it. The red sea steamed under the rain outside, the rusty fog coiling languidly through the open arches of the gallery. Rann watched them lazily from a raised couch set massively into the wall. Her long sparkling legs sprawled arrogantly across the black spider-silk draperies. This time her tabard was a pale yellow. Her eyes were still the color of shoal-water, still amused, still secret, still dangerous.

Starke said, "So you made me do it after all."

"And you're angry." She laughed, her teeth showing white and pointed as bone needles. Her gaze held Starke's. There was nothing casual about it. Starke's hawk eyes turned molten yellow, like hot gold, and did not waver.

Beudag stood like a bronze spear, her forearms crossed beneath her bare sharp breasts. Two of Rann's palace guards stood behind her.

Starke began to walk toward Rann.

She watched him come. She let him get close enough to reach out and touch her, and then she said slyly, "It's a good body, isn't it?"

Starke looked at her for a moment. Then he laughed. He threw back his head and roared, and struck the great corded muscles of his belly with his fist. Presently he looked straight into Rann's eyes and said:

"I know you."

She nodded. "We know each other.

Kelly Freas, illustration for "Lorelei of the Red Mist," from *Tops in Science Fiction,* fall 1953. (© Love Romances Publishing Co., Inc./Fiction House, 1953)

ABOVE: Virgil Finlay, original artwork for title illustration of "A Sound of Thunder," from *Senior Scholastic*, November 1953. (© *Senior Scholastic* magazine, 1953)

LEFT: Artist unknown, title illustration for "The Golden Apples of the Sun," from *Planet Stories*, November 1953. (© Love Romances Publishing Co., Inc./Fiction House, 1953)

Stanley Meltzoff, title illustration for "The Illustrated Man," from *Esquire,* July 1950. It may be said of Stanley Meltzoff that never has a commercial artist who has produced so few paintings influenced so many people over such a long period of time. Only a small percentage of his paintings were used for science fiction paperback covers: Robert Heinlein's *Puppet Masters, The Green Hills of Earth, Tomorrow, the Stars,* and Alfred Bester's *The Demolished Man.* However, thanks to these few science fiction covers and the time he spent teaching at Brooklyn's Pratt Institute, he had a profound influence on a younger generation of artists. Richard Powers, Paul Lehr, John Schoenheer, and Vincent Di Fate have all expressed gratitude for Meltzoff's original paintings of the 1950s. Ray Bradbury has acknowledged the contributions that luck and timing have made to his own career; it would seem that Stanley Meltzoff's acceptance of the *Esquire* assignment to illustrate *The Illustrated Man* was an example of such luck. (© *Esquire* magazine, 1950)

LEFT: Al Parker, title illustration for "The World the Children Made," from *The Saturday Evening Post,* September 1950. (© *The Saturday Evening Post* 1950)

RIGHT: Michael Mitchell, title illustration for "The Rocket Man," from *Maclean's Magazine,* March 1951. (© *Maclean's Magazine,* 1951)

LEFT: James R. Bingham, title illustration for "The Beast from 20,000 Fathoms," from *The Saturday Evening Post,* June 1951. (© *The Saturday Evening Post,* 1951)

As Bradbury began to move beyond the pulp magazines, the illustrations commissioned for his stories grew in scale, and benefited from an infusion of new artistic talent and an explosion of color. Slick magazine artists were sometimes given full pages for a lead illustration, and the quality of reproduction was top drawer. Gone were the yellowing pages of the pulps, with their low-grade reproductions of black-and-white illustrations. Taking their place was a fresh burst of color and an entirely unique group of illustrators, some of whom, including Ben Shahn and Stanley Meltzoff, already enjoyed national reputations.

The April Witch · By RAY BRADBURY

She'd broken his heart once, but now he knew her for what she was. She could never hurt him again—he thought.

Tom placed his lips to the strange mouth and he kissed her. He was trembling.

ILLUSTRATED BY GEORGE GARLAND

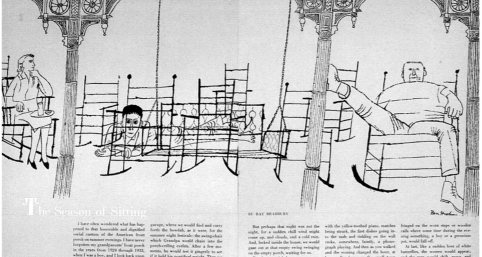

The Season of Sitting

BY RAY BRADBURY

ABOVE LEFT: James Bingham, title illustration for "Bullet with a Name," from *Argosy,* April 1953. (© All Fiction Field [Popular], 1953)

ABOVE RIGHT: George Garland, title illustration for "The April Witch," from *The Saturday Evening Post,* April 1952. (© *The Saturday Evening Post,* 1952)

LEFT: Ben Shahn, title illustration for "The Season of Sitting," from *Charm,* August 1951. (© *Charm* magazine/Ben Shahn Estate, 1951)

AN INTERPRETATION OF RAY BRADBURY'S CHRISTMAS STORY—"THE GIFT"

PAINTED ESPECIALLY FOR ESQUIRE BY REN WICKS

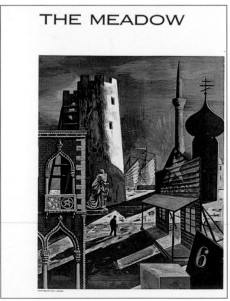

Frederick Siebel, title illustration for "A Sound of Thunder," from *Collier's,* June 1952. (© *Collier's* magazine, 1952)

James Bingham, title illustration for "The Rocket Man," from *Argosy,* February 1952. (© All Fiction Field [Popular], 1952)

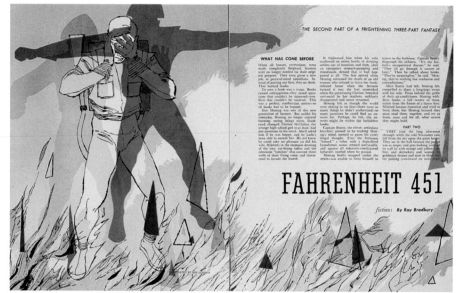

RIGHT: Franz Altschuler, title illustration for "A Sound of Thunder," from *Playboy,* June 1956. (© HMH Publishing Co., Inc., 1956)

BELOW: Bruce Johnson, title illustration for "Shopping for Death," from *Maclean's,* June 1954. (© *Maclean's* magazine, 1954)

James R. Bingham, original art for "The Beast from 20,000 Fathoms," from *The Saturday Evening Post*, June 1951. (© *The Saturday Evening Post*/James Bingham estate, 1951)

OVERLEAF TOP: James Bama, title illustration for "The Beggar on the Dublin Bridge," from *The Saturday Evening Post*, January 1961. (© *The Saturday Evening Post*, 1961)

OVERLEAF, FAR LEFT: Al Hirschfeld, title illustration for "The Prehistoric Producer," from *The Saturday Evening Post*, June 1962. (© *The Saturday Evening Post*, 1962)

OVERLEAF CENTER: Keats, title illustration for "The Machineries of Joy," from *Playboy*, December 1962. (© HMH Publishing Co., Inc., 1962)

OVERLEAF LEFT: Amos Sewell, title illustration for "Summer in the Air," from *The Saturday Evening Post*, February 1956. (© *The Saturday Evening Post*, 1956)

These two photographs of convention book displays show the diversity of small-press and professional hardcover publications during the 1950s. Bradbury's *Dark Carnival,* published by Arkham House, is barely visible in the top photograph (front row, second from the far left), and in the bottom photograph (second row in, to the far left, just beside Robert E. Howard's *Skullface and Others*). The 1950s saw the rise of independent small press publishers committed specifically to science fiction and fantasy literature, as well as early experimentation in science fiction by some of the larger and more well-known houses, such as Doubleday Books, Crown, Ballantine Books, and Harcourt, Brace and Company. (Photograph courtesy of the collection of Forrest J Ackerman. © Forrest J Ackerman, 2002)

TOP: *Writers' Markets & Methods,* vol. 58, no. 3 (March 1948). (© *Writers' Markets & Methods,* 1948)

BOTTOM: This advertisement, for a book signing at John Valentine Books in Glendale, CA, to promote *The Golden Apples of the Sun,* appeared in the May 1953 issue of fanzine *Science-Fiction Advertiser.* (© Roy A. Squires, 1953)

CHAPTER

3

To Hardcovers and Paperbacks

Photograph © Glynn Crain, 2001

Ray Bradbury began the 1950s by moving from the small specialty publisher Arkham House, which had just released his first hardcover collection, *Dark Carnival* (in 1947), to the mainstream publisher Doubleday & Company. With the release of *The Martian Chronicles*, Bradbury was catapulted from the status of a cult favorite among science fiction readers to that of a famous author, read throughout the world. It is ironic that Doubleday would reject the manuscript for *Fahrenheit 451*, thus leading the young author into an important relationship with the legendary publishing duo of Ian and Betty Ballantine of Ballantine Books. As a result, Ballantine would release the perennially popular *Fahrenheit 451* and, eventually, *The October Country*—both classic books graced by remarkable, timeless cover and interior artwork by Joseph Mugnaini. When Bradbury resumed his publishing relationship with Doubleday, he insisted that the notation "Science Fiction" not appear on his books' spines, and from thenceforward his books were published as "mainstream" titles, outside the traditional Doubleday science fiction list.

It was at the beginning of this period of time that Bradbury met and began his lifelong creative relationship with Joseph Mugnaini.

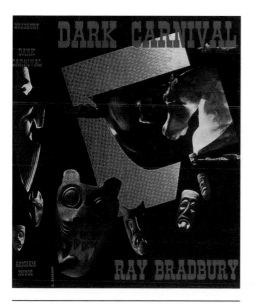

George Barrows, cover design for *Dark Carnival*, Arkham House, 1947. George Barrows was a California photographer who incorporated a combination of wooden masks and photography in the design of Bradbury's first hardcover book. (© Arkham House, 1947)

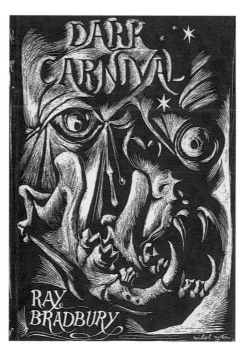

Michael Ayrton, cover artwork for *Dark Carnival* (British edition), first published in 1948. (© Hamish Hamilton, 1948)

Arthur Lidov, original painting for cover of *The Martian Chronicles,* 1950. During the 1950s, Arthur Lidov was an accomplished painter of abstract paintings who lived on Long Island. He had published illustrations in *Life* magazine, and had exhibited his paintings in New York City. The choice of the cover artwork for this important first mainstream book by Bradbury was entirely in the hands of Doubleday & Company staff, and Bradbury himself never liked this cover. Almost immediately thereafter Bradbury began to exert his own ideas and taste in relation to cover artwork for his titles. (© Doubleday & Company, Inc., 1950)

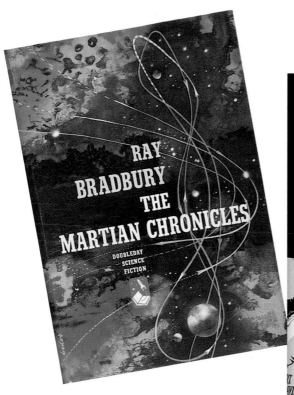

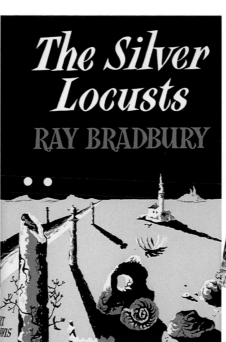

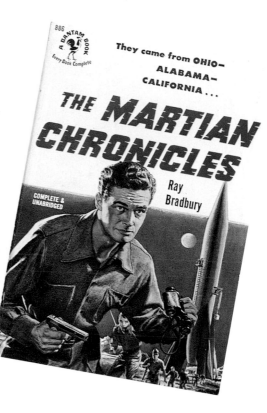

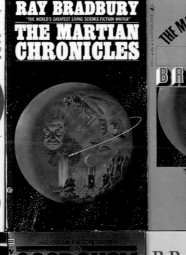

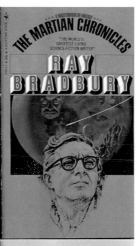

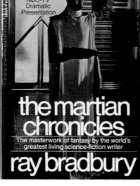

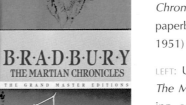

ABOVE LEFT: Arthur Lidov, cover illustration for *The Martian Chronicles,* 1950. (© Doubleday & Company, Inc., 1950)

ABOVE CENTER: Roy Sanford, cover illustration for *The Silver Locusts* (British-only title of *The Martian Chronicles*), 1951. (© Rupert Hart Davis, 1951)

ABOVE RIGHT: *The Martian Chronicles* (Bradbury's first U.S. paperback). (© Bantam Books, 1951)

LEFT: U.S. paperback versions of *The Martian Chronicles,* including covers by Ian Miller and Michael Whelan. (© Bantam Books, 1954–91)

ABOVE: Michael Whelan, *Destiny's Road,* acrylic on watercolor board, original cover artwork for the fortieth-anniversary edition of *The Martian Chronicles,* 1991. Many Bradbury enthusiasts consider this to be the definitive *Martian Chronicles* cover. (© Bantam Books/Doubleday/Michael Whelan estate, 1989–2002)

INSET: *The Martian Chronicles,* large-print edition. (© G. K. Hall & Company, 1989)

LEFT: John Richards, original painting for cover of *The Silver Locusts* (British-only title of *The Martian Chronicles*), 1956. John Richards was the art editor for *Authentic Science Fiction Monthly,* one of the top English sf digest magazines during the early 1950s. He did the paintings for many of the *Authentic* covers, and later expanded into a career as paperback cover artist. (© Corgi Books, 1956)

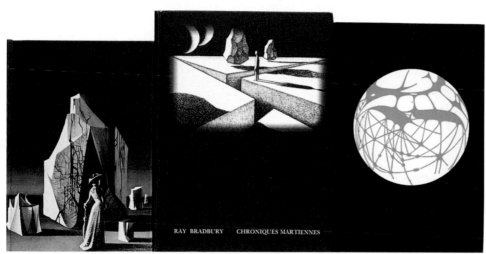

ABOVE LEFT: Endpaper, *Chroniques Martiennes* (France). Special interior endpaper sculpture design model by Jacques Noël for the first French edition *The Martian Chronicles*. (© Le Club du Meilleur Livre [book club limited edition], 1955)

ABOVE RIGHT: Dust jacket, *The Martian Chronicles*. Special promotional design for the 1988 TV adaptation of *The Martian Chronicles,* most likely wrapped around the current Bantam edition of the paperback and distributed at promotional events in Los Angeles. This variant design would see no further distribution anywhere else in the country. (Image courtesy of the collection of Donn Albright. © Channel 4–KNBC/Bantam Books, 1988–89)

CENTER LEFT: *Chroniques Martiennes* (France). Early French hardcover editions of *The Martian Chronicles*. (© La Bibliotheque de Culture Literaire/Editions Denoël/Le Club du Meilleur Livre, 1955)

BOTTOM LEFT: Foreign paperback editions of *The Martian Chronicles: Crónicas Marcianas* (Argentina), *Martanská Kronika* (Czechoslovakia), *Die Mars-Chroniken* (Germany). (© Editiones Minotauro/Circulo de Lectores/Circulo de Lectores/Mlada Fronta/Wilhelm Heyne Verlag, München/Izdevniecíba Zinátne, Riga, 1967/Európa Könyvkiadó 1982/Európa Könyvkiadó, 1982/Science Fiction—Roman Erzäblungen/Editiones Minotauro, 1965–85)

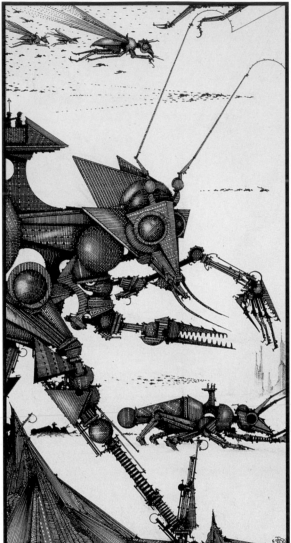

ABOVE LEFT: Ian Miller, privately commissioned color specialty work for *The Martian Chronicles* for *Rocket Summer, January 1999.* (Image courtesy of the collection of Glynn Crain. © Ian Miller, 1979)

ABOVE RIGHT: Ian Miller, interior art for *The Martian Chronicles,* titled *February 1999: Yalla.* (Image courtesy of the collection of Glynn Crain. © Ian Miller, 1979)

RIGHT: Photograph of Ray Bradbury in his basement writing studio, around 1955–56. (Photograph by Lou Jacobs Jr., courtesy of the collection of Ray Bradbury. © Lou Jacobs Jr./Courtesy of the collection of Ray Bradbury, 1955–56)

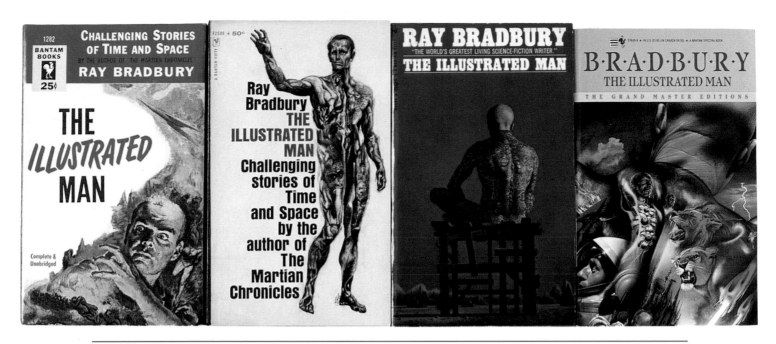

ABOVE: U.S. paperback editions of *The Illustrated Man,* including cover artwork by Jim Burns. (© Bantam Books, 1952–95)

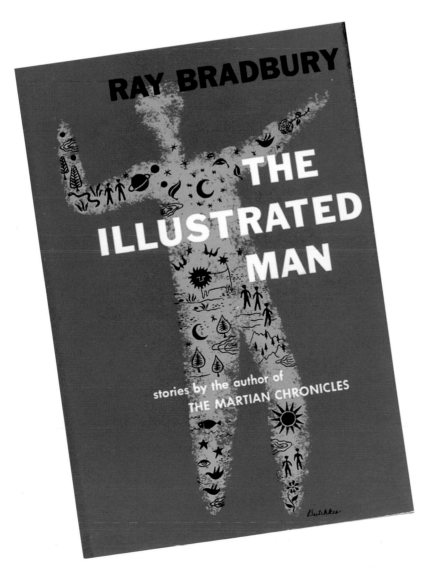

LEFT: Sydney Butchkes, cover design for *The Illustrated Man,* first American edition, 1951. (© Doubleday & Company, Inc., 1951)

BELOW: John Minton, cover design for *The Illustrated Man* (British), first hardcover edition. (© Rupert Hart-Davis, 1952)

LEFT: Ian Miller, original artwork for paperback cover of *The Golden Apples of the Sun,* pen and ink with watercolor on illustration board, 1978. From the boxed set with matching covers by Ian Miller released in 1978. (Image courtesy of the collection of Glynn Crain. © Bantam Books, 1978; Ian Miller, 2002)

BELOW: Ian Miller, original artwork for the alternate paperback cover of *The Golden Apples of the Sun,* pen and ink with watercolor on illustration board, 1978. Ian Miller's more recent paperback covers have won rave reviews from Bradbury fans and readers. (© Bantam Books, 1978; Ian Miller, 2002)

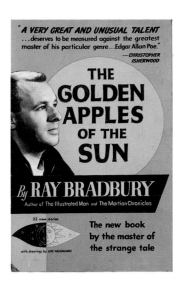

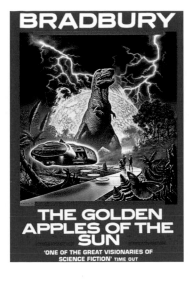

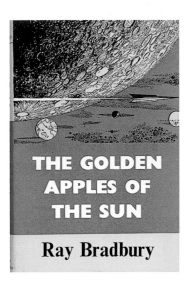

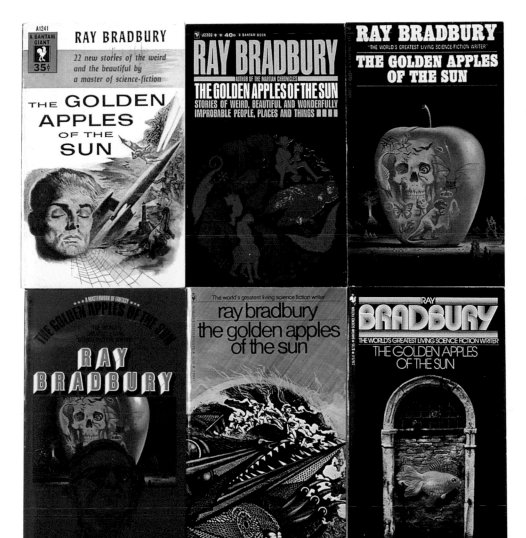

ABOVE, FAR LEFT: Original unused cover for *The Golden Apples of the Sun,* with cover artwork by Joseph Mugnaini. This cover was saved from obscurity by longtime Bradbury collector Donn Albright, who, upon a visit to the Bantam Books editorial offices in the 1960s, noticed a shelf copy with an unfamiliar spine. It is unclear why this cover was not used. (Cover courtesy of the collection of Donn Albright. © Bantam Books, 1954)

SECOND TO LEFT: Advance publicity poster for *The Golden Apples of the Sun,* Doubleday Books. Posters such as this were used for book signings or for display in retail stores. (© Doubleday & Company, 1953)

SECOND FROM RIGHT: British paperback edition of *The Golden Apples of the Sun.* (© Corgi Books/Panther Books Ltd., 1955–97)

ABOVE: *The Golden Apples of the Sun* (British), cover artwork and interior drawings by Joseph Mugnaini. (© Rupert Hart-Davis, 1953)

LEFT: U.S. paperback editions of *The Golden Apples of the Sun.* (© Bantam Books, 1954–96)

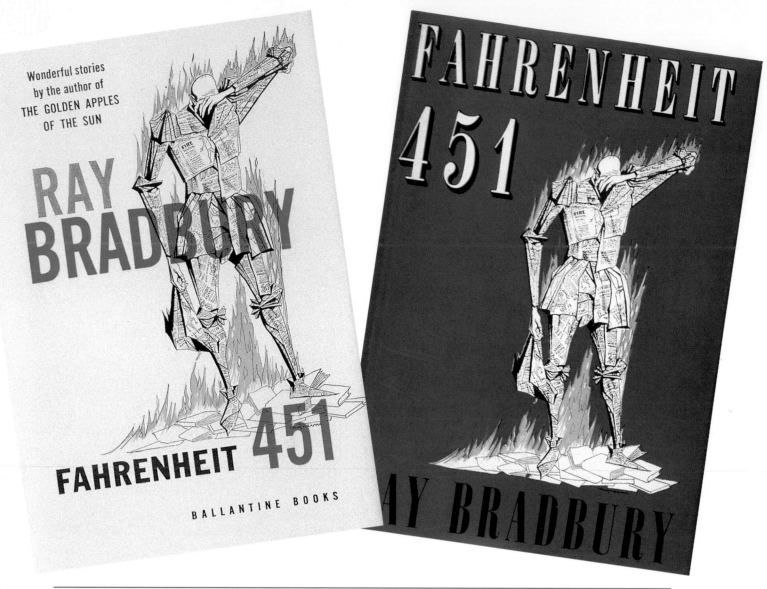

LEFT: *Fahrenheit 451,* first Ballantine hardcover printing, cover artwork by Joseph Mugnaini. (© Ballantine Books, Inc., 1953)

RIGHT: *Fahrenheit 451,* first British hardcover printing, cover artwork by Joseph Mugnaini. (© Rupert Hart-Davis, 1954)

Mugnaini illustrated many of Bradbury's important early books and, throughout his career, Bradbury has maintained a keen interest in the design and cover artwork for all his work. This chapter maps out the creative evolution of Bradbury's book covers, from early hardcover first editions, to the later mass-produced paperback editions, to foreign editions, to original artwork that was commissioned for special reprint titles.

Having left behind the pulp magazines for the newer commercial product of paperback books, Bradbury eventually became one of the most widely read authors in America. Along the way he remained loyal to his pulp roots, even as his style was maturing and evolving, securing for Bradbury a revered position in American letters.

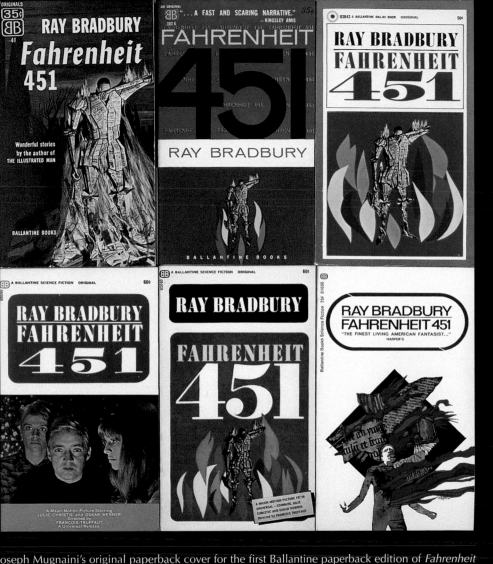

Joseph Mugnaini, original artwork for the first hardcover edition of *Fahrenheit 451*, pen and ink with brush on illustration board, Double-day & Company, 1953. (Image courtesy of the collection of Ray Bradbury. © Joseph Mugnaini estate/Doubleday & Company, 1953)

Joseph Mugnaini's original paperback cover for the first Ballantine paperback edition of *Fahrenheit 451* is a masterpiece. Throughout the history of science fiction and fantasy, there are few examples of a major work of fiction being published with an accompanying masterpiece cover painting. A worthy candidate might be Isaac Asimov's original *I Robot*, with its stunning and simple Edd Cartier painting. Others might point to the original publication of *The Hobbit*, with drawings and cover illustration by author J. R. R. Tolkien, as a prime example of excellence. Richard Powers's powerful wraparound cover painting for Arthur C. Clarke's *Childhood's End* also comes to mind, as does the Ace paperback cover by John Schoenherr for Frank Herbert's *Dune*. Joseph Mugnaini's cover for

ABOVE LEFT: British paperback editions of *Fahrenheit 451*. British artist John Richards painted a very close tribute to the Mugnaini's original U.S. cover. (© Corgi Books/Panther Books, 1957–76.)

ABOVE: Foreign editions of *Fahrenheit 451*: *451 Stupnu Fahrenheita* (Czechoslovakia), *Fahrenheit 451* (Austria), *451 Grads Pec Farenheita* (Latvia/USSR), *Fahrenheit 451* (Norway). (© Svobodné Slovo Melantrich/Buchergilde Gutenberg, Vienna/ Izdevniecíba Zinátne, Riga/Tornserien Norstedts/Pax Forlag Als, Oslo, 1960–80)

LEFT: Foreign paperback editions of *Fahrenheit 451*: Denmark, Japan, Denmark, Italy, Italy, Germany. (© Spektrums Pocket-boger/Hayakawa/ Gyldendals Traneboger/Arnoldo Mondadori Editore/Arnoldo Mondadori Editore/Heyne Büchuer)

Foreign paperback editions of *Fahrenheit 451*: *Fahrenheit 451* (Spain), *451° Fahrenheita* (Poland), *451°Fahrenheit* (Romania), *Fahrenheit 451* (Netherlands, Spain, Norway, Spain). (© Plaza & Janes/Cytelnik, 1960/Editura Tineretului/Het Spectrum, Prisma Science Fiction, 1971/Rota Tiva, Plaza & Janes, S.A. Editores, 1977/Pax Forlag Als, Oslo/Ediciones Orbis, S.A. [Spain], 1960–80)

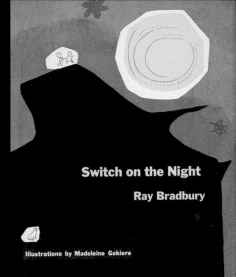

Switch on the Night, first hardcover edition, with illustrations by Madeleine Gekiere. The first book that Bradbury wrote for children. (© Pantheon Books, 1955)

In the mid-1950s, Shasta publisher and editor Mel Korshak contacted Ray Bradbury requesting a contribution for a proposed anthology of science fiction stories entitled *Let's Ride a Rocket*. Korshak was an old friend of Bradbury; the two had begun their association upon meeting at the first World Science Fiction Convention in 1939. His small science fiction press, Shasta Publishers, was one of the most important of its time, publishing work by authors such as Robert Heinlein and L. Ron Hubbard, among many others. *Let's Ride a Rocket* was conceived to attract juvenile readers, a market that boasted a healthy readership. Bradbury submitted "Subterfuge," and the project made it as far as galley proofs but went no further, as Shasta postponed the project, then ran out of funds. The cover comprehensive sketch ("comp") was done by Mel Hunter.

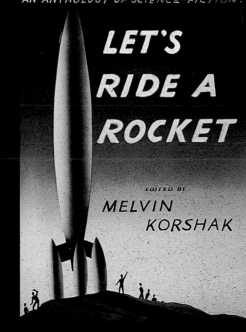

Let's Ride a Rocket, unpublished cover artwork. (© Mel Korshak, Shasta Publishers,

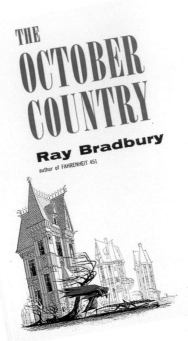

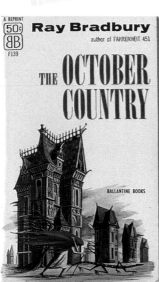
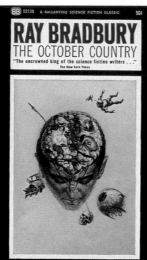
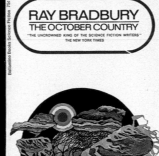

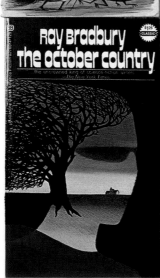

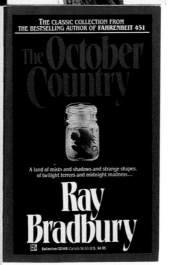

ABOVE LEFT: Joseph Mugnaini, hardcover for *The October Country*, gouache, watercolor, and pen and ink, and on illustration board. This cover echoes the mood established with *Fahrenheit 451,* and established Mugnaini as *the* Bradbury artist for the 1950s and beyond. (© Ballantine Books, Inc., 1955)

ABOVE CENTER AND RIGHT: Joseph Mugnaini, preliminary sketches for the cover of *The October Country,* watercolor on illustration board, 1955. (© Joseph Mugnaini estate)

LEFT: U.S. paperback editions of *The October Country.* (© Ballantine Books, Inc., 1954–72)

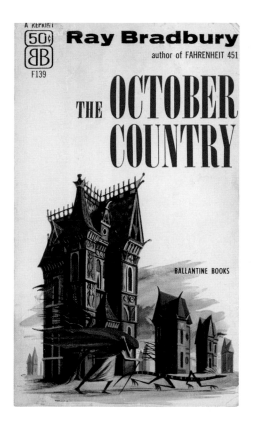

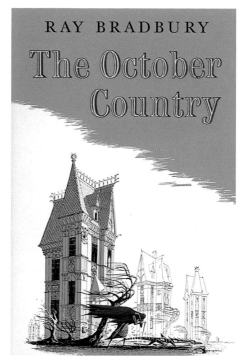

FAR LEFT: Joseph Mugnaini, cover and interior illustrations for *The October Country,* first paperback edition. (© Ballantine Books, Inc., 1956)

LEFT: *The October Country*: the first British hardcover edition also carried the Mugnaini illustrations. (© Rupert Hart-Davis, 1956)

British paperback editions of *The October Country.* (© Ace Books/Four Square/NAL/Panther Books and Grenada, 1961–92)

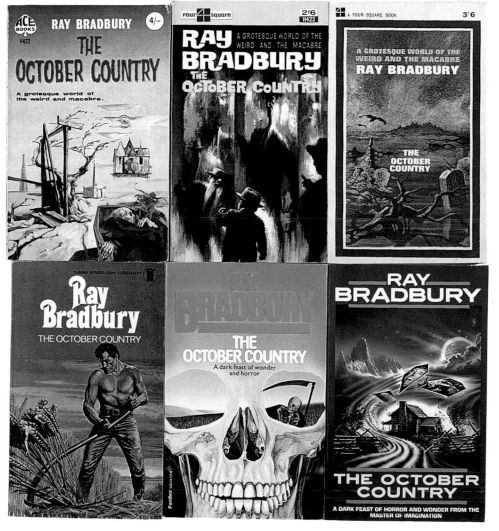

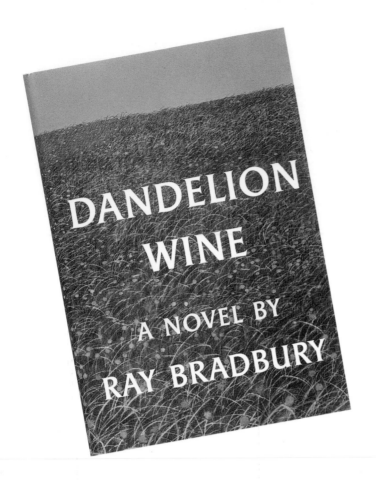

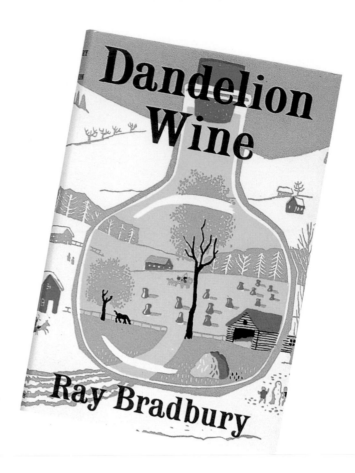

TOP LEFT: *Dandelion Wine*, first American hardcover edition, jacket design by Robert Vickery. (© Doubleday & Company, Inc., 1957)

TOP RIGHT: *Dandelion Wine*, first British hardcover edition, jacket design by Jeffery Lies. (© Rupert Hart-Davis, 1957)

ABOVE: U.S. paperback editions of *Dandelion Wine*, including cover artwork by Tom Canty. (© Bantam Books, 1959–92)

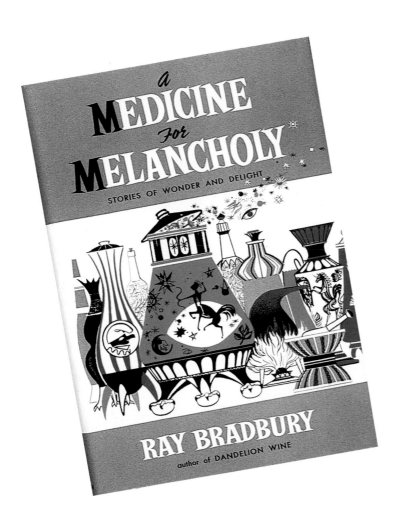

TOP LEFT: *A Medicine for Melancholy,* jacket design by Joseph Mugnaini. (© Doubleday & Company, Inc., 1959)

TOP RIGHT: *The Day It Rained Forever* (British-only title of *A Medicine for Melancholy*), with jacket design by Joseph Mugnaini. (© Rupert Hart-Davis, 1959)

ABOVE: U.S. paperback editions of *A Medicine for Melancholy.* (© Bantam Books, 1960–86)

Gray Foy, original artwork for *Something Wicked This Way Comes*, gouache on illustration board. (Photograph courtesy of the collection of Ray Bradbury. © Simon & Schuster, 1962)

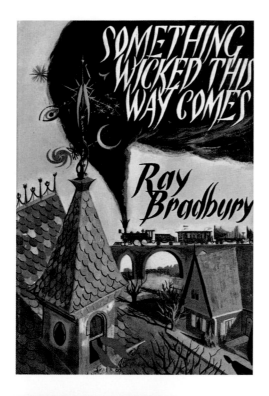

Something Wicked This Way Comes (British), jacket design by Joseph Mugnaini. This dust jacket design by Mugnaini will forever remain special to Ray Bradbury. Bradbury was first exposed to the artist's work when he saw a painting (The Caravan) that he felt was visually prophetic of the story told in Something Wicked This Way Comes. When Bradbury completed the novel, Mugnaini was commissioned to create the dust jacket painting. At this point Bradbury sent Joe the preliminary painting (see page 171) he had done and had Mugnaini finish the cover. (© Rupert Hart-Davis, 1963)

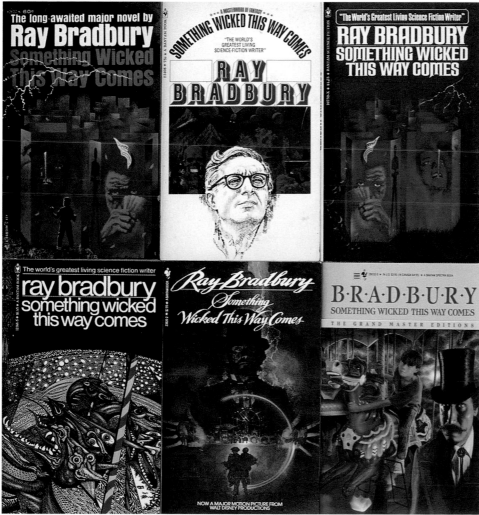

U.S. paperback editions of Something Wicked This Way Comes. (© Bantam Books, 1963–92)

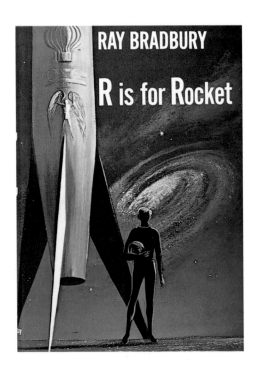

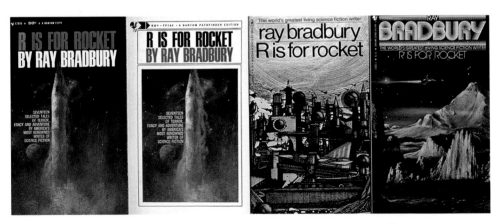

TOP: Ian Miller, original artwork for the British paperback edition of *R Is for Rocket*, pen and ink with watercolor on illustration board. (© Corgi Books, 1976/Ian Miller, 2002)

ABOVE: U.S. paperback editions of *R Is for Rocket*. (© Bantam Books, 1966–89)

LEFT: Hardcover edition of *R Is for Rocket,* jacket design by Joseph Mugnaini. (© Doubleday & Company, Inc., 1962)

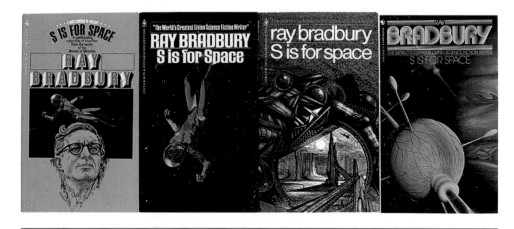

TOP: Ian Miller, original artwork for American paperback edition of *R Is for Rocket,* pen and ink with watercolor on illustration board. (© Bantam Books, 1978/Ian Miller 2002)

ABOVE: U.S. paperback editions of *S Is for Space.* (© Bantam Books, 1970–86)

RIGHT: *S Is for Space,* first hardcover edition, jacket design by Joseph Mugnaini. (© Doubleday & Company, Inc., 1966)

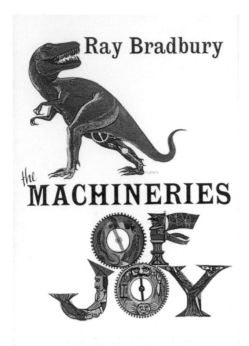

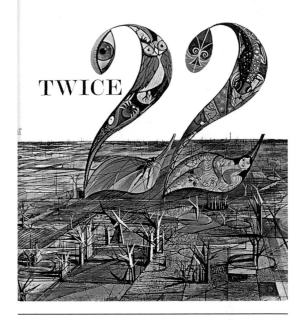

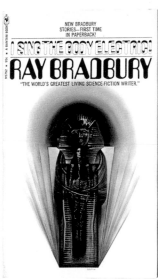

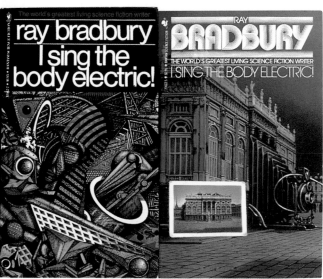

Ian Miller, original artwork for *Long After Midnight,* pen and ink with watercolor on illustration board, 1977. (© Bantam Books, 1978)

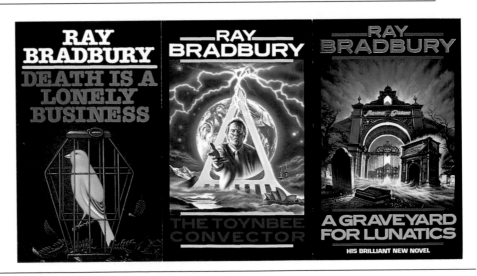

ABOVE: British paperback editions of *Death Is a Lonely Business, The Toynbee Converctor,* and *A Graveyard for Lunatics.* (© Grafton and Granada, 1986–93)

LEFT: *The Halloween Tree,* first hardcover edition, jacket design and interior illustrations by Joseph Mugnaini. (© Alfred A. Knopf, 1972)

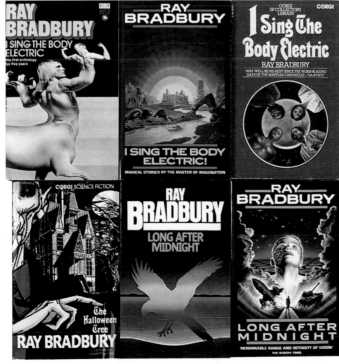

ABOVE: U.S. paperback editions of *Writers' Voices—Selected from Dark They Were and Golden-Eyed*, *Dinosaur Tales*, *The Complete Poems of Ray Bradbury*, *A Memory of Murder*, *Green Shadows, White Whale*, *A Graveyard for Lunatics*, *The Toynbee Convector*, and *Death Is a Lonely Business*. (© Bantam Books/Dell/ Ballantine Books, 1970–90)

LEFT: British paperback editions of *I Sing the Body Electric, The Halloween Tree*, and *Long After Midnight*. (© Corgi Books, 1971–91)

Ray Bradbury and Joe Mugnaini

Ray Bradbury first came upon the work of Joseph Mugnaini when he and his wife, Maggie, were walking one day in Venice, California. As they passed the display window of a small gallery Bradbury noticed a lithograph of an old house that was like nothing he had ever seen before. He entered the gallery to inquire about the piece, and was told he could have it for seventy-five dollars—much more than he could afford at the time. However, he was told, he could make payments over time.

However, the gallery owner led Bradbury into another room. There hung a much larger version of the lithograph—a rich, vibrant painting of the Victorian haunted house that completely overwhelmed him. How much was this painting? Just $250, he was told (again, time payments could be arranged). Beside this painting was another, and when the young Bradbury gazed upon it he experienced a "metaphoric vision." This second painting depicted a uniquely designed train traveling high upon a trestle. Passengers rode inside and atop the train as it roared through a fantasy landscape. The track behind the train was broken, and the track before it led nowhere. As Bradbury gazed at the painted train, he realized that he was working on story ideas that held a parallel metaphor (stories which would later lead to the novel *Something Wicked This Way Comes*).

Although he declined to purchase the painting, Bradbury asked the gallery owner if it was possible to have the artist's phone number. As soon as possible, Bradbury called Joseph Mugnaini and introduced himself; the two would soon become fast friends and soul mates for life. Bradbury expressed his admiration for Mugnaini's work and proposed the following: if the paintings did not sell in the show, would it be possible for Bradbury to buy both *Modern Gothic* and *The Caravan*? Bradbury also asked for a discount of 50 percent, knowing that most galleries took one-half of the asking price as commission; he felt this way he could afford the paintings and not deprive the artist of any of his potential income.

A month later a call came into the Bradbury home. "Come get your paintings," Joe Mugnaini said. It was only later that Bradbury learned that Mugnaini had pulled these very two paintings out of the show, and had kept them available so that they could be sold *only* to Ray Bradbury.

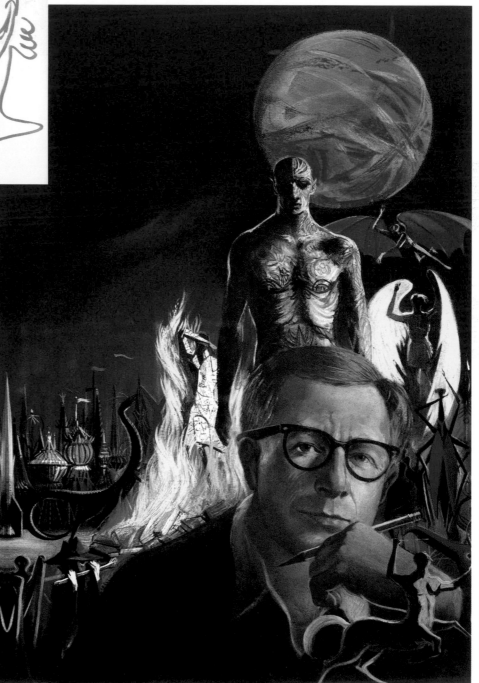

LEFT: A letter from Ray Bradbury to Joseph Mugnaini, dated June 8, 1991. Note Bradbury's own "doodle." Bradbury often embellishes his personal correspondence with whimsical drawings.

BELOW: Joseph Mugnaini, original cover artwork for the May 1963 special "Ray Bradbury Issue" of *The Magazine of Fantasy and Science Fiction.* (© Mercury Press, Inc., 1963)

ABOVE: Joseph Mugnaini, original preliminary watercolor cover sketch for the May 1963 special "Ray Bradbury Issue" of *The Magazine of Fantasy and Science Fiction.* (© Joseph Mugnaini estate, 2002)

TOP LEFT: Joseph Mugnaini, original preliminary sketch for *Fahrenheit 451,* 1991. This version was done for the Easton Press special edition. (© Joseph Mugnaini estate, 1991)

TOP RIGHT: Joseph Mugnaini, larger preliminary painting for Easton Press edition of *Fahrenheit 451.* (© Joseph Mugnaini estate 1991)

ABOVE LEFT: Joseph Mugnaini, preliminary watercolor designs for *Fahrenheit 451,* 1953. (Images courtesy of the collection of Ray Bradbury. © Joseph Mugnaini estate, 1953)

ABOVE RIGHT: Joseph Mugnaini, preliminary watercolor sketch for *Fahrenheit 451,* 1953. At the time Mugnaini was working on early cover concepts for *Fahrenheit 451,* Bradbury knew he wanted to retitle "The Fireman" (the title under which the original story was first published in *Galaxy Magazine*). Bradbury would eventually call the Los Angeles Fire Department to inquire, "At what temperature does paper burn?" The answer, of course, provided the novel's title. At this juncture, Bradbury may have already told Mugnaini (and the artist forgot the exact number), or he may have said he'd "soon" have a final title, and to use any number at hand for the early sketches. (© Joseph Mugnaini estate, 1953)

LEFT: Joseph Mugnaini, original black-and-white illustration for *The Martian Chronicles,* 1974. This illustration was used in the Limited Editions Club (Avon, Connecticut) offering for 1974. (© The Cardavon Press/Joseph Mugnaini estate, 1974)

RIGHT: Joseph Mugnaini, original black-and-white illustration for "A Sound of Thunder," from *The Golden Apples of the Sun,* 1953. (© Doubleday Books/Joseph Mugnaini estate, 1953)

LEFT: Joseph Mugnaini, original black-and-white illustration for *The Martian Chronicles,* 1974. The illustration was used in the Limited Editions Club offering for 1974. (© The Cardavon Press/Joseph Mugnaini estate, 1974)

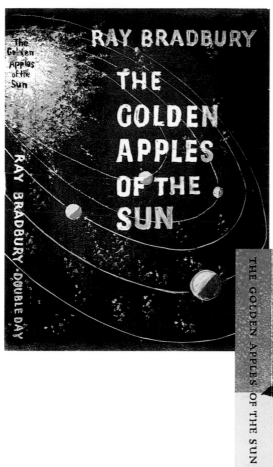

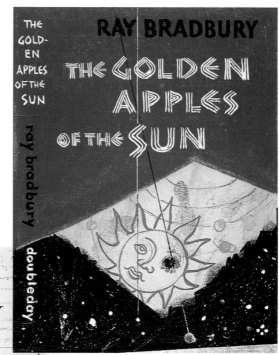

LEFT, RIGHT, BELOW RIGHT, BELOW LEFT: Joseph Mugnaini, original preliminary paintings for unused covers of *The Golden Apples of the Sun,* 1953. (Image courtesy of the collection of Ray Bradbury. © Joseph Mugnaini estate, 2002)

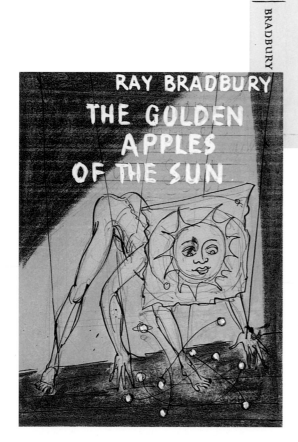

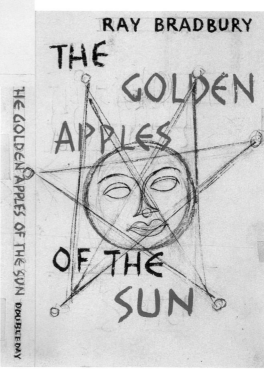

ABOVE CENTER: Joseph Mugnaini, original color painting design (turned in to printer as color guide) for the cover of *The Golden Apples of the Sun,* 1953. (Image courtesy of the estate of Joseph Mugnaini, © Doubleday Books/Joseph Mugnaini estate, 1953)

ABOVE: Joseph Mugnaini, original black-and-white illustration for the Doubleday first edition of *The Golden Apples of the Sun*, 1953. (© Doubleday Books/Joseph Mugnaini estate, 1953)

LEFT: Joseph Mugnaini, original illustration for "The Fog Horn," from *The Golden Apples of the Sun*, 1953. (© Doubleday Books/Joseph Mugnaini estate, 1953)

ABOVE: Joseph Mugnaini, original illustration for "The Wind," from *The October Country,* 1955. (© Ballantine Books/Joseph Mugnaini estate, 1955)

ABOVE RIGHT: Joseph Mugnaini, original illustration for "The Cistern," from *The October Country,* 1955. (© Ballantine Books/Joseph Mugnaini estate, 1955)

RIGHT: Joseph Mugnaini, original illustration for "The Dwarf," from *The October Country,* 1955. (© Ballantine Books/Joseph Mugnaini estate, 1955)

ABOVE LEFT: Joseph Mugnaini, original lithograph illustration for *Fahrenheit 451,* The Limited Editions Club, 1982. (© The Limited Editions Club, Inc., 1982)

ABOVE CENTER: Joseph Mugnaini, original lithograph illustration for *The Martian Chronicles,* The Limited Editions Club, 1974. (© The Cardavon Press, Inc., 1974)

ABOVE RIGHT: Joseph Mugnaini, original preliminary watercolor sketch for the cover of *R Is for Rocket,* 1962. (Image courtesy of the collection of Donn Albright. © Joseph Mugnaini estate, 2002)

LEFT: Joseph Mugnaini, original preliminary painting for *Fahrenheit 451,* offered by The Limited Editions Club, watercolor on board, 1982. This stunning collector's edition was bound in aluminum by Robert A. Burlen & Sons, Hingham, Massachusetts. (Image courtesy of the collection of Donn Albright. © Joseph Mugnaini estate, 2002)

ABOVE LEFT: Joseph Mugnaini, original preliminary watercolor sketch for *The Day It Rained Forever*, 1959. (Image courtesy of the collection of Donn Albright. © Joseph Mugnaini estate, 2002)

ABOVE RIGHT: Joseph Mugnaini, original preliminary watercolor sketches for *The Day It Rained Forever*, 1959. (Image courtesy of the collection of Ray Bradbury. © Joseph Mugnaini estate, 2002)

LEFT: Joseph Mugnaini, original preliminary painting for *The October Country*, 1955. (Image courtesy of the collection of Ray Bradbury. © Joseph Mugnaini estate, 2002)

ABOVE LEFT: Joseph Mugnaini, *The Green Morning,* original lithograph from the limited and signed portfolio *Ten Views of the Moon,* 1981. (© Lynton Kistler, Los Angeles, 1981)

ABOVE RIGHT: Joseph Mugnaini, *Halloween,* original lithograph from the limited and signed portfolio *Ten Views of the Moon,* 1981. (© Lynton Kistler, Los Angeles, 1981)

FAR LEFT: Joseph Mugnaini, *A Tower on Mars,* original lithograph from the limited and signed portfolio *Ten Views of the Moon,* 1981. (© Lynton Kistler, Los Angeles, 1981)

LEFT: Joseph Mugnaini, *The Visitor,* original lithograph from the limited and signed portfolio *Ten Views of the Moon,* 1981. (© Lynton Kistler, Los Angeles, 1981)

BELOW LEFT: Joseph Mugnaini, *A Martian Town,* original lithograph from the limited and signed portfolio *Ten Views of the Moon,* 1981. (© Lynton Kistler, Los Angeles, 1981)

ABOVE: Joseph Mugnaini, original black-and-white illustration for *The Halloween Tree*, 1972. (© Alfred A. Knopf/Joseph Mugnaini estate, 1972)

LEFT: Photograph of Joseph Mugnaini and Ray Bradbury at the opening of an exhibit of Mugnaini's artwork, early 1960s. (Photo courtesy Diana Robinson, the estate of Joseph Mugnaini. © Joseph Mugnaini estate, 2002)

CHAPTER 4

EC Comics and Ray Bradbury: The Untold Story

Photograph © Glynn Crain, 2001

The story of how Ray Bradbury came to have his writing adapted by a small, energetic company named Entertaining Comics in the 1950s is now a legendary chapter of comics history. Yet even though some people are familiar with the cast of characters, and many more have knowledge of Bradbury's past accomplishments, this part of the author's career is still often shrouded in misconceptions and misunderstandings. But, in the 1970s, the discovery of a group of letters written between Ray Bradbury and EC Comics publisher Bill Gaines would shed new light on this fascinating chapter of Bradbury's career.

By 1951, publisher Bill Gaines and his primary editor, Al Feldstein, had already used four uncredited Ray Bradbury stories as "springboards" for stories in their horror and science fiction comic book titles. In the March/April 1951 issue of *The Haunt of Fear* (No. 6) they used Bradbury's "The Handler," modifying it slightly and retitling it as "A Strange Undertaking." Later in the same year, in the December

OVERLEAF: Frank Frazetta, cover painting for *Tomorrow Midnight*, the second Ballantine paperback containing reprints of Bradbury's EC stories. This painting was Frazetta's second attempt at the cover. After seeing his first try, Ian Ballantine suggested changes that led Frazetta to decide to make a completely new painting. One of the most noticeable differences between the first and second versions is the man's near-nude state in the original. (Original paperback cover © Ballantine Books, 1966; painting © Frank Frazetta estate, 2002. Used with permission)

LEFT: Al Williamson, cover artwork for *Weird Science-Fantasy* No. 25 (Sept. 1954), featuring the Bradbury story "A Sound of Thunder." This was one of only two EC covers featuring artwork based directly on the Bradbury story within. The other was *Weird Fantasy* No. 20, which featured a scene from "I, Rocket" rendered by EC editor and artist Al Feldstein. (© William M. Gaines, Agent, Inc., 1954. Used with permission)

1951/January 1952 issue of *The Vault of Horror* (No. 22), they clipped "The Emissary," and changed it into "What the Dog Dragged In." And in the May/June 1952 issue of *Weird Fantasy* (No. 13), Gaines and Feldstein used two more Bradbury stories, "Kaleidoscope" and "The Rocket Man," and transformed them into "Home to Stay."

It is common knowledge that Gaines and Feldstein used a large number of authors and their work as sources of ideas for their comic book titles. A color photo taken at the original Lafayette Street offices during a 1951 Christmas party shows Bill Gaines and Al Feldstein leaning on a door frame next to a shelf full of bound comic volumes, books, and a stack of *Weird Tales* pulp magazines. Because the horror comic titles were the mainstay of EC's publishing line, it would seem reasonable to suppose that they were also reading the Arkham House books published by August Derleth in Wisconsin, and the other pulp magazine titles of the time, including *Planet Stories,* published by rival Fiction House. Here they would have come across Bradbury's early work in abundance.

Eventually some of Bradbury's friends noticed the EC swipes and brought them to his attention. In a letter dated April 19, 1952, Bradbury wrote:

Dear Sir:

Just a note to remind you of an oversight. You have not as yet sent on the check for $50.00 to cover the use of secondary rights on my two stories THE ROCKET MAN and KALEIDOSCOPE which appeared in your WEIRD-FANTASY May-June '52 #13, with the cover-all title of HOME TO STAY. I feel this was probably overlooked in the general confusion of office-work, and

Johnny Craig (left) and Al Feldstein (right) looking over Bill Gaines's shoulder as he inspects EC cover artwork, early 1950s. Both Craig and Feldstein, already EC artists, would become EC editors as well during this time period. This photo was taken before EC received its first letter from the young Ray Bradbury. (Photograph courtesy of the collection of Cathy Gaines Mifsud. © Cathy Gaines Mifsud and EC Publications Inc.)

look forward to your payment in the near future. My very best wishes to you.

Yours cordially,
Ray Bradbury

P.S. Have you ever considered doing an entire issue of your magazine based on my stories in DARK CARNIVAL, or my other two books THE ILLUSTRATED MAN and THE MARTIAN CHRONICLES? I'd be very interested in discussing this with you for some future issue. I think we could do an outstanding job here. May I hear from you? If you wish, I could send copies of my books on for perusal. R. B.

Gaines and Feldstein must have been both relieved and flattered that Bradbury chose to write a letter that gave them the benefit of the doubt (albeit while making it clear, through humor, that he knew exactly what was going on). At the same time, he invited them to make amends through proper arrangements for future adaptations. It is unlikely that either Gaines or Feldstein had read or seen the recently printed *Ray Bradbury Review*, authored and published by longtime Bradbury fan William F. Nolan in San Diego in 1952. It is also extremely unlikely that either Gaines or Feldstein had ever tripped across a copy of the *Fantasy Advertiser* and noticed ads placed by one Ray Bradbury, requesting specific Sunday newspaper *Tarzan* comics. If they had read these fan publications they would have been clued into Bradbury's long-standing love of magic, magicians, carnivals, and comic strips. In a somewhat guarded return letter dated April 25, 1952, Gaines and Feldstein wrote:

Dear Mr. Bradbury,

We are extremely flattered to learn that you feel our "Home to Stay," which appeared in Weird Fantasy, *May–June, 1952, #13, is an adaptation of your two stories, "The Rocket Man" and "Kaleidoscope." Although we do not agree with your conclusions, we are completely disinclined to quibble with one who writes as charming a letter as yours . . . so we are enclosing our check for $50.00, without intending to agree with your contentions.*

We are most happy to learn that you are a reader of Weird Fantasy. *We have read several of your stories in the past, and have nothing but the very greatest of admiration for you and for your writings. We, too, would be most interested in working with YOU, and enthusiastically invite you to drop in and chat about it the next time you are in New York. Or, if you are planning no visit in the near future, please write and let us know how we can get together.*

> *Very cordially,*
> *William M. Gaines, Managing Editor*
> *Albert Feldstein, Editor*

The guarded nature of the Gaines and Feldstein letter seemed to suggest that they were caught in the act, were willing to comply with Bradbury's request for payment, but didn't want to confess entirely! Regardless, the Bradbury/EC partnership was about to begin.

Bill Gaines's father, M. C. "Max" Gaines, was one of

Wally Wood, splash-page artwork for "Home to Stay!" from *Weird Fantasy* No. 13 (May–June 1952). By 1952, Wally Wood was entering into his mature inking style. "Home to Stay!" would be the first Bradbury story that would be assigned to Wood from 1952 though 1954. This story—a combination of "Rocket Man" and "Kaleidoscope"—was the first acknowledged (if after the fact) Bradbury story by Feldstein and Gaines. The earliest full-story swipe is "What the Dog Dragged In," from "The Emissary," in *Vault of Horror* No. 22 (Dec. 1951–Jan. 1952). (© William M. Gaines, Agent, Inc., 1952. Used with permission)

the original pioneers in the comic book field. Responsible for packaging and promoting the first comic book in 1934, entitled *Famous Funnies*, Gaines Sr. was eventually made editor and publisher for All-American Comics, in partnership with DC Comics. He helped create such influential titles as *All-American Comics, Flash Comics,* and *Wonder Woman;* however, by 1945 he decided to sell out his interests in these titles to the parent company, DC Comics. After his split with DC he formed his own company, Educational Comics, and began printing titles (some of which were left to him from DC Comics) with names like *Picture Stories from the Bible, Picture Stories from Science,* and *Animal Fables.*

He eventually began to experiment with more popular themes and during 1946–47 introduced *International Comics, Land of the Lost, Moon Girl and the Prince,* and others. These comics were being published from his offices at 225 Lafayette Street, just above Little Italy and Chinatown in New York City. At this point fate would step in and deal an unexpected turn of events to comics history and Ray Bradbury's own career.

On August 20, 1947, Bill Gaines received a phone call from his uncle Will informing him that Max had died in a boating accident while vacationing at Lake Placid, New York. The younger Gaines, nearly finished with a degree in chemistry at New York University, was now made the head of Educational Comics at his mother's insistence. It was not long before Gaines began to make changes.

His first important decision was to hire an artist named Al Feldstein. Feldstein had recently brought in his portfolio of "good-girl" artwork (comics that took the Archie Andrews teenage theme an adult step further, with gorgeous, sexy young women, drawn in a strong linear style) in hopes of impressing the new publisher. Bill quickly discovered that his new artist could write as well as he could draw, and the two of them began to make changes to the content of the Educational Comics line. They altered the company name to Enter-

Al Feldstein, re-creation painting titled *Weird Fantasy No. 11 Revisited.* Al Feldstein consigned his first EC cover re-creation to Sotheby's 1991 Comic Art Auction. He has continued to enjoy strong fan support and commissions over the past decade, repainting many of his best original EC covers. (Painting © Al Feldstein, 1995)

taining Comics, and began a new line of titles such as *Modern Love, Crime Patrol, War Against Crime,* and *Saddle Justice.* Gaines wanted to take advantage of Feldstein's talent for drawing women, and the romance titles featured stories like "I Had Two Husbands!" and "I Was a 'B' Girl!" It was within the crime comics, however, that Gaines and Feldstein sprang their first revolutionary idea. At the end of 1949, they introduced the "Horror Hosts" the Crypt Keeper and the Vault Keeper, in *Crime Patrol* and *War Against Crime* respectively, as vehicles to tell modern horror stories. At this point, the struggling new line of comics was just barely beginning to show some profit, but as the sales figures began to come in for their experiment in horror (and the letters began to flood the offices), Bill Gaines and Al Feldstein saw their future unfolding before them. It was during this very period that they must have first begun to use *Weird Tales, Planet Stories,* and other pulp magazines as source material for their issues. During this time they undoubtedly read the young author Ray Bradbury, whose short stories stood out from the crowd and almost seemed to beg for adaptation into comic book form.

By 1952 EC was transformed from a secondary line of titles with a struggling distribution history to front runners in the business, setting trends and causing the entire comics industry to follow their lead. Since horror comic titles like *Tales from the Crypt* were making so much money, there was room for experimentation, and Gaines and Feldstein both had a soft spot for science fiction. They created *Weird Fantasy* and *Weird Science* to augment their titles *The Haunt of Fear* and *The Vault of Horror.* They now had a well-rounded stable of titles, and dropped their romance comics to focus on crime, horror, adventure, and science fiction themes. Al Feldstein was now editing many of these titles and realized the multidimensional quality of an author like Ray Bradbury who was writing both horror and science fiction short stories. Their star was on the rise, and they intended to take Ray Bradbury with them. Bradbury was quick to reply to their April 25 letter, responding on April 28, 1952:

Dear Mr. Gaines & Mr. Feldstein:

Thanks for your prompt check in payment for use of my stories in your good magazine; it was much appreciated.

I enclose copies of my two books, THE MARTIAN CHRONICLES *and* THE ILLUSTRATED MAN, *and hope you will consider these for possible projects in the future. I think that the* CHRONICLES *especially would make a fine one-issue project for you people, doing the entire book, with a few deletions here or there,*

Al Feldstein, original cover artwork for *Weird Fantasy* No. 11 (Jan.–Feb. 1952). This cover drew its inspiration from a 1947 painting by Chesley Bonestell used to illustrate an article in a 1948 issue of *Collier's Magazine.* (© William M. Gaines, Agent, Inc., 1952. Used with permission)

in a single issue of your magazine WEIRD FANTASY, *or perhaps putting out a special one-shot magazine titled* ROCKETS TO MARS! *which I think could have a tremendous sale for you people, since science-fiction is a wildly growing field these days. I am vitally interested in seeing my book become a single comic-book issue because I believe it is the first step toward starting the younger readers on their way to reading my work later, in the Bantam or Doubleday editions. It has been my experience that reading magazines such as yours amply whets an appetite that grows by the year.*

Unfortunately, I do not plan on visiting New York this year, but I would like to get into this project in more detail with you, and if you think it an exciting one, as I do, I'm sure we could arrange

all details to our mutual satisfaction through my agent Don Congdon of the Harold Matson Agency in New York. In the meantime, while the project is still nebulous, it would be interesting to kick ideas back and forth across the country about this. If you are interested, I know a young artist-cartoonist whose work I would like to show you, and there are a number of ideas that could be gone into. May I hear from you as soon as you have time to read the enclosed books? Many many thanks!

Yours cordially,
Ray Bradbury

It is interesting to note that Bradbury here was already suggesting a prophetic comic book format, not realized in its entirety till the late 1960s and 1970s by the comics industry as the comic-novel, or the graphic novel. EC would soon experiment with "theme-based" comic books that held to one idea or historical series of events when

Harvey Kurtzman wrote the Civil War and Korean War "theme" issues for *Frontline Combat* and *Two-Fisted Tales*. It is possible that Bill Gaines remembered his father's stunning commercial failures with large "theme-based" comic books (e.g., *Picture Stories from the Old Testament*, etc.) when he replied to Bradbury on May 16, 1952:

Dear Mr. Bradbury:

Thanks ever so much for the two sets of autographed books. Both Al and I were delighted with them. We've read through the remaining stories which we had not read previously . . . as well as devouring a copy of Dark Carnival!

To try and produce any one of your volumes as a "single" comic issue of 28 pages of art and story would be impossible. Also, I feel it would be a risky venture financially . . . as the majority of our readers, being readers of comics, probably never heard of you—and the titles aren't "punchy" enough!

However, I have a counter proposal which I sincerely believe would benefit both you and us greatly! First let me sketch in a few facts about EC. We introduced both horror and "real" science fiction into the field in January of 1950—about 2½ years ago. We've been widely imitated, but still retain the readership in both fields. We've built up a huge faithful readership, as demonstrated by the few letters (out of hundreds we receive each week!) which I enclose.

So here's what we propose to do for you! Run an adaptation of one of your weird or science stories (for which we'd pay you $25 each!) in every issue, or almost every issue, of our horror and science fiction mags, giving you a byline with full credit for plot—such as "Adapted from 'Such and Such' by Ray Bradbury"—and possibly featuring your name on the covers! In addition, we would give you a big play in the popular editorial columns of our magazines, plugging your books and various ventures! Our total print order on one round of the three horror mags, two science fiction mags, and Shock SuspenStories *for this coming July–August period will be 2,650,000—our horror mags sell over 80%, while the other three sell in the 70's! Believe me when I say that we could do a "plugging" job! And an "honest" one, too, as both Al and I have long been admirers of yours . . . and sincerely believe you to be just about tops in the entire fantasy field.*

We, on the other hand, would not only derive top-notch plot material from such an arrangement, but the prestige value of your name—which if it doesn't mean too much to our readers now, would in the course of a few months of plugs!

I enclose copies of our present nine titles for your inspection—all are bimonthlies with print orders ranging from 350,000 to 500,000.

I truly believe that we could have a delightful and mutually profitable association. So now let's hear from you, so we can put this into full swing as soon as possible!

> *Very Cordially,*
> *William M. Gaines, Man. Ed.*

Gaines was certainly correct that previous science fiction comic titles had held very little serious content. His only real competition came from Bradbury's former agent, Julius Schwartz. Schwartz, a longtime science fiction fan, was now an editor at DC Comics, and had recently begun using *Strange Adventures* and *Mystery in Space* to showcase stories adapted from authors such as Edmond Hamilton, Otto Binder, and Gardner Fox. Bill Gaines's suggestion that the Bradbury name could be run on the covers as an additional plug must have flattered the young author, and would later lead to unforeseen developments. The letters now began to fly back and forth. Bradbury wrote on May 19:

Dear Bill Gaines:

Thanks for your very pleasing and stimulating letter and the packet of magazines you sent on. Your offer seems mighty interesting, and I have, in turn, air-mailed your letter on to my agent, Don Congdon, at the Harold Matson Agency in New York. He'll probably be in touch with you this week to see what can be arranged for the future. I believe we can do each other a lot of good both ways, and your suggestion that you do one story an issue (or thereabouts), rather than an entire issue of my material, seem very sensible. By all means, keep in touch with me; I'll be in touch with my agent, and

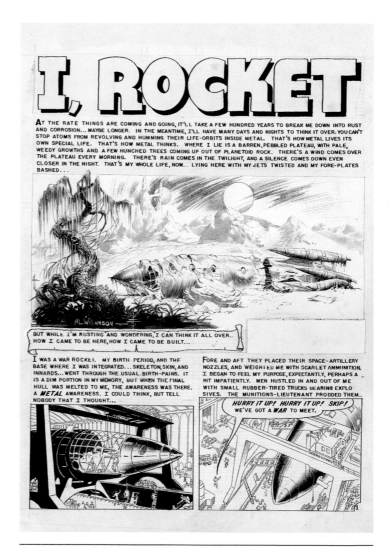

Al Williamson, splash-page artwork for "I, Rocket," from *Weird Fantasy* No. 20 (July–Aug. 1953). This splash page also featured the initials "FF" as a signature and was one of the only times that Frank Frazetta took credit for helping the young Al Williamson with an EC story assignment. Bradbury has stated many times that Al Williamson was one of his favorite EC artists. (© William M. Gaines, Agent, Inc. 1953. Used with permission)

ABOVE: Wally Wood, splash-page artwork for "There Will Come Soft Rains," from *Weird Fantasy* No. 17 (Jan.–Feb. 1953). (© William M. Gaines, Agent, Inc., 1953. Used with permission)

ABOVE RIGHT: Wally Wood, page 2 artwork for "There Will Come Soft Rains," from *Weird Fantasy* No. 17 (Jan.–Feb. 1953). (© William M. Gaines, Agent, Inc., 1953. Used with permission)

between all of us, I'm sure we'll have a bang-up good time. Again thanks for your stimulating interest! My best to you and Al!

Yours,

Ray B.

In a letter dated May 22, 1952, Bradbury's agent, Don Congdon, wrote in part:

Dear Mr. Gaines:

Ray Bradbury turned over to me your letter about your desire to use some of his stories as the basis for comic strips. We certainly agree

that they are excellent springboards for such exploitation. This agency has been handling Ray's work with the book and magazine markets and all the allied subsidiary markets. . . .

. . . Actually, Bradbury shouldn't be an unknown name to the buyers of comic books off the newsstand—I mean that two of his volumes have been done by Bantam Books and have sold upwards of a quarter of a million copies each. In addition, magazines like The Saturday Evening Post *and* Collier's *have done a number of his stories.*

I'd like to discuss this further with you. Would you give me a ring at your convenience?

Sincerely,

Don Congdon

The exchange of words over circulation numbers seems to have reinforced Don Congdon's opinion that Bradbury deserved a better license fee.

As the letters continued to flow between Bradbury and Gaines during May, June, and July, the two worked out problems with story copyrights, artist assignments, and biographical information that EC was requesting for future issues. Bradbury sent Gaines a copy of *The Ray Bradbury Review* in June of 1952. Gaines requested and received permission from Don Congdon to use stories previously published in *Weird Tales* and *Planet Stories*. As the first stories began to appear in the EC comics titles, Bradbury wrote in part on August 18, 1952:

Dear Bill:

By all means, please show this letter to Jack Davis and Joe Orlando. I want to thank them for the painstaking work they did on THE COFFIN, *and* THE LONG YEARS. *I got a great deal of pleasure looking at the silver prints of the first two adaptations. Thanks so much for sending them on! And please thank Al for the fine layout work and the adaptations themselves! This is a real adventure for me!*

LEFT: Wally Wood, page 4 artwork for "There Will Come Soft Rains," from *Weird Fantasy* No. 17 (Jan.–Feb. 1953). (© William M. Gaines, Agent, Inc., 1953. Used with permission)

ABOVE: Wally Wood, page 6 artwork for "There Will Come Soft Rains," from *Weird Fantasy* No. 17 (Jan.–Feb. 1953). "There Will Come Soft Rains" stands out among EC Bradbury story adaptations for its exclusive use of narration. This story does not contain a single word balloon, and the spatial freedom given to Wally Wood allowed him to turn in a masterpiece of comic art. (© William M. Gaines, Agent, Inc., 1953. Used with permission)

You ask for criticism, and I have only one minor gripe, which may or may not please you to hear about. For what it is worth, here it is. Would there be any chance, in the future, of cutting down on the exclamation points?!!!!!!!

Otherwise, I have nothing but the kindest regard and love for you, Al, Mr. Orlando, and Mr. Davis, for work beautifully and

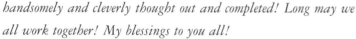

handsomely and cleverly thought out and completed! Long may we all work together! My blessings to you all!

Yours,
Ray

And again on August 24, Bradbury wrote in part:

Dear Bill:

. . . Thanks for your accompanying note. The points you make are certainly worth making, and I appreciate your taking the time to make them. The comic business (or the business of reading and noting the peculiarities of comic style, anyway) is not unfamiliar to all of us. To explain this remark, let me say that I have been a fervent collector of comic strips and panels since the age of 8 in 1928 when Buck Rogers first started. I have a complete file of BUCK ROGERS daily strips from 1928 through 1937, all BR Sunday panels from 1930 through 1937, FLASH GORDON from 1934

ABOVE LEFT: Joe Orlando, page 1 artwork for "The Long Years," from *Weird Science* No. 17 (Jan.–Feb. 1953). Joe Orlando stated on several occasions that he was as proud of his Bradbury adaptations as of anything he had done in the comics medium. (© William M. Gaines, Agent, Inc. 1953. Used with permission)

ABOVE RIGHT: Bill Gaines at his desk at the offices of *MAD* magazine, circa the mid-1970s. Photograph by E. B. Boatner. (Courtesy of E. B. Boatner. © E. B. Boatner, 2002)

through 1938, PRINCE VALIANT from 1937 through 1952, and TARZAN (drawn by Harold Foster) from 1932 through 1936, plus hundreds of old POPEYES, OUT OUR WAYS, ALLEY OOPS, etc. My big dream, when I was a kid, was to be a magician or a cartoonist or a hambone actor. I didn't become any of those, though I've had experience in major or minor form, in all those fields. So my interest, you see, in your staff, your magazines, and in you, is not a passing one at all. . . .

ABOVE: Al Feldstein, re-creation painting titled *Weird Fantasy No. 17 Revisited*. From the collection of Dr. Richard Hauser, original editor of the EC fanzine *Spa-Fon*. (Painting © Al Feldstein, 2002)

RIGHT: Al Feldstein, original cover artwork for *Weird Fantasy* " No. 17" (despite cover notation, in actuality this was No. 5, Jan.–Feb. 1951). (© William M. Gaines, Agent, Inc., 1951. Used with permission)

And again in October 15, 1952, in part:

This first paragraph can only go to thank George Evans for his superb drawing of THE SMALL ASSASSIN and to Jack Davis for his swell work for LET'S PLAY POISON! You people have a way of continually making me happy. I can't thank you enough. . . .

And again on November 10, 1952:

. . . MARS IS HEAVEN and ZERO HOUR are very fine, very fine indeed. Please give your best handshake all around to everyone on these. Thanks to all of you for the time and energy you spent. Al, Mr. Wood, and Mr. Kamen!

Thanks for the "writeup" you got from the fan mag, also. And for the letters you sent on, reacting to your announcement of the Bradbury adaptations. This is heartening. . . .

I enclose the biographical sketch you asked for. I hope you will forgive me if I suggest that you publish this sketch exactly as I have written it. . . .

Again I want to thank all of you for the continual job of doing well by me, that you are doing. I sincerely hope to see all of you when I come to New York, probably next year. . . .

On November 17, 1952, Bradbury sent the first letter to EC Comics addressed to individual artists:

Dear Wally Wood and Jack Kamen:

Just a personal and private word to both of you, including my thanks and gratitude for the really beautiful work you are doing on my stories. This is an entire new experience to me, and I cannot tell you enough how much I appreciate the painstaking detail and thought you are putting into your effort. I was particularly pleased and delighted with the new ones: MARS IS HEAVEN and ZERO HOUR. It seemed to me that again and again you both achieved the exactly right atmosphere and angle in carrying out the story. Thanks again and my good wishes to you and everyone at EC.

Yours with admiration,
Ray Bradbury

By December 5, 1952, Bradbury was addressing issues that would explain why certain stories were never adapted for EC though many would have thought it an editorial decision upon the part of Al Feldstein:

Dear Bill:

. . . I hadn't realized that McCall's and Saturday Evening Post and Harper's were holding out on us. You might ask Don to ask these people again, on my behalf, to release rights. God knows, they can be stubborn, in which case there's nothing we can do. Ditto Street and Smith and Standard. All we can do is keep asking, over a period of time. . . .

Yours, as ever,
Ray

Now we come to the moment in Bradbury's relationship with EC Comics that represents a dilemma faced by many writers. During the 1950s, however, this problem was unique to Bradbury.

Although it would be another two years before Fredric Wertham's book *Seduction of the Innocent* would be published, and the same period of time before Bill Gaines would appear before the Senate Subcommittee to Investigate Juvenile Delinquency (hearings held in New York City to examine the comic industry and the material it published), it seemed that all of a sudden horror comics were coming under attack from parents' groups, educational institutions, and the news media. Bradbury himself was just beginning to enjoy the respectability and critical favor that came from having his fiction published in the slick magazines; he was well aware that continuing to publish in the lowly pulp magazines put his career at risk. Most authors would have cut and run, preferring to play it safe. Looked at within the context of the times, Bradbury made a compassionate and brave decision that

Bernard Krigstein, page 1 artwork for "The Flying Machine," from *Weird Science-Fantasy* No. 23 (March 1954). "The most arresting imagery in Bradbury's original version of 'The Flying Machine' is not the machine—a flimsy, kitelike contraption of colored paper—but the emperor's miniature world, set in motion by a key and controlled by a clockwork mechanism. Krigstein's visualization of the story delicately expresses the point of Bradbury's image: that the country over which the emperor rules is as much an artificial construct as the table top model. The many long shots, beginning with the splash panel, suggest that we are looking not at the Chinese landscape but at a tiny replica, preserved inviolate under a glass dome and too exquisitely arranged to be convincingly real. The characters suggest dolls arranged in a series of tableaux, and the seizure and beheading of the flier—the only violent acts in the story—take place between the panels."—Bill Mason, excerpted from *Weird Science-Fantasy*, reprint vol. 1, by Russ Cochran, publisher. (© Russ Cochran Publisher, 1982. © William M. Gaines, Agent, Inc. 1952. Used with permission)

ABOVE: Bernard Krigstein, page 3 artwork for "The Flying Machine," from *Weird Science-Fantasy* No. 23 (March 1954). When he first viewed this Feldstein/Krigstein effort for the adaptation of "The Flying Machine," Ray Bradbury commented that he had never seen finer work from a comic artist. (© William M. Gaines, Agent, Inc., 1952. Used with permission)

ABOVE RIGHT: Bernard Krigstein, page 4 artwork for "The Flying Machine," from *Weird Science-Fantasy* No. 23 (March 1954). (© William M. Gaines, Agent, Inc., 1952. Used with permission)

now stands as a testament to his love of the comics medium, as the McCarthy era was coming into full bloom and criticism of the popular arts was about to explode.

As can be seen in the following letters, Bradbury held his ground during this dark period of American cultural history. But although courageous, his actions are not surprising. After all, he was about to begin writing *Fahrenheit 451,* titled for the temperature at which paper burns:

January 25, 1953

Dear Bill:

This is one of those difficult letters which "hurts me more than it does you." I hope, anyway.

It seems that the world is full of niggling, critical, carping, nasty, trouble-making people. Either that is true, or I am growing rapidly into the neatest case of paranoia on record. It seems that there are many "friends" just waiting around, with nothing else to do but juggle innuendo, knife one in the back, or make strategic withdrawals and attacks. I've seen a lot of it in the past year, in my own career, small as it is. I've seen a lot more in the past month. The latest reaction, unpleasant and unsettling, has centered around the EC COMICS association with one R. Bradbury, an association I have found to be of the friendliest. An association that has been cooperative in the extreme. Your adaptations of my work have been faithful and exact, you have utilized my narrative and my dialogue. I have had no reason to feel that you have laid rough hands

ABOVE LEFT: Severin and Elder, page 1 artwork for "The Million Year Picnic," from *Weird Fantasy* No. 21 (Sept.–Oct. 1953). (© William M. Gaines, Agent, Inc., 1953. Used with permission)

ABOVE RIGHT: Severin and Elder, page 5 artwork for "The Million Year Picnic," from *Weird Fantasy* No. 21 (Sept.–Oct. 1953). One of Bradbury's letters to Bill Gaines specifically requests the services of Severin and Elder for the upcoming adaptation of "The Million Year Picnic." Bradbury was impressed with the Severin/Elder renditions of children, and felt the blending of their talents resulted in the perfect artistic sensibility for this story. (© William M. Gaines, Agent, Inc., 1953. Used with permission)

on any of my work, and, as you know, I have expressed my thanks to you and your artists time and again for your friendly attitude and work well-done. Much thought and sweat has gone into your work there in New York.

Yet I have seen the beginnings of the usual, and this time amplified, criticism all about, here in L.A., from friends, and from busi-

ness acquaintances at the studios. I won't quote them at length. The consensus of opinion is that Bradbury is now writing for the comics and the world has come to an end, or some such drivel as that. Even though I have pointed out to many many people that your work is an adaptation of mine and that I have simply let you proceed to do all of the work yourself, the rumbles have not subsided, and, in particular, there has been much comment on the appearance of my name on the covers of the horror comics where the cover illustrations themselves have not been, shall we say, "pleasant"?

Needless to say I have been upset, irritated, and angered at all this. It was not a thing I considered at the time we began our association. The whole association seemed like it was going to be a lot of fun, and it has been enjoyable to me right on down the line.

Nevertheless, the future must be considered, and as a businessman (for when I am away from my typewriter I try to sell my work as steadily and as shrewdly as possible, which is a rarity in a writer), I must think over all of my contracts for the coming year.

In the light of these carping, niggling, nasty criticisms (many of them, I am sure caused by nothing more than a hidden form of jealousy), I have decided to ask you good people to do me a tremendous favor, and I hope you will help me at this time. Could you possibly eliminate my name from the covers of your comic magazines as soon as possible?

By all means, continue with your adaptations, exploit my stories and my name INSIDE your magazines, all that you wish. You will have my fullest cooperation. In all of your magazines, you can forecast the coming of my stories in your other publications, in letters six inches high, if you wish. But I hope you can see your way clear

to taking my name off the cover of the weird comic magazines by the end of April or some time in May, and doing the same thing, in your science fiction comic magazines by the end of May or some time in June, thus giving you a leeway of some months in which you will have plenty of time to let your readers know that Bradbury will appear steadily with you during the coming year. Then when you drop my name from the covers, your readers will know that in future issues they will find my work inside, and will instinctively look to see if each issue contains a new one by yours truly.

I have debated writing this letter to you for several weeks, for I find the whole business embarrassing and silly, but I have finally

ABOVE LEFT: Severin and Elder, page 6 artwork for "The Million Year Picnic," from *Weird Fantasy* No. 21 (Sept.–Oct. 1953). (© William M. Gaines, Agent, Inc., 1953. Used with permission)

ABOVE RIGHT: Severin and Elder, page 7 artwork for "The Million Year Picnic," from *Weird Fantasy* No. 21 (Sept.–Oct. 1953). (© William M. Gaines, Agent, Inc., 1953. Used with permission)

ABOVE: Al Feldstein, cover artwork for *Weird Fantasy* No. 13 (May–June 1952). The Mars of Percival Lowell and Ray Bradbury looms above the spacemen on this famous EC science fiction cover. (© William M. Gaines, Agent, Inc., 1952. Used with permission)

ABOVE RIGHT: Wally Wood, page 1 artwork for "Mars Is Heaven," from *Weird Science* No. 18 (Mar.–Apr. 1953). This adaptation offered EC editor Al Feldstein one of the few occasions to include a classic "EC Snap-Ending" within the narrative of the original Bradbury short story. (© William M. Gaines, Agent, Inc., 1953. Used with permission)

decided that something must be done, and I know you will understand that the pressure of this business had forced my action at this time. My work spreads itself among people at all levels, I have had letters from eight year olds and from professors at Balliol, Oxford, from Christopher Isherwood and Edmond Hamilton, from Gerald Heard and Jessamyn West and from Jack Smith in Sweetwater, Ohio. I know that W. H. Auden and Dylan Thomas like it and I know that Bob Jones of Waukeshaw likes it. All of these levels and

interests must be considered. I want to entertain them all, if I can. You have helped me to entertain a lot of people at many age-levels in your magazines, and I want to go on with this, if you, in turn, are willing. But in order to forestall some of the growing criticism, the name will have to be dropped from the covers. I'll have to do my entertaining, in your publications, behind the curtain.

I hope that this letter does not, in turn, irritate, unsettle, or anger you too much. I hope that you will understand how reluctant I have been to write you at all. And I hope that all of you know how much I have appreciated your hard work in my behalf in the past months.

Please let me hear from you on this by return air-mail, Bill. I realize that many of your covers are made up, with my name on them, for two or three months ahead, so I do not expect immediate action. But by your April, May, or June issues, if you can help me out, I would be in your debt very much. All my best wishes to all of you.

Yours,

Ray

Al Feldstein with Roy Krenkel and Al Williamson, cover artwork for *Weird Fantasy* No. 18 (March–April 1953). The small box which read "In This Issue: E.C.'s Adaptation of a Story by RAY BRADBURY, America's Top Science-Fiction Writer!" would eventually lead to problems for the young author, who was about to leap from the pulps into slick magazines and was beginning a career in Hollywood. (© William M. Gaines, Agent, Inc., 1953. Used with permission)

Bill Gaines answered almost immediately in a letter dated Wednesday, January 28, noted at the top as "Late evening—at home!":

Dear Ray—

To get to first things first, rest assured that your perfectly reasonable request has not and will not affect our delightful association one whit!

Now to go back and start over! First, my sincere apologies for

not having written lately—we have been snowed under with work—and I'm finally writing this before hitting the sack at home, because two days have slipped past since yours of the 25th arrived, and I'll be disturbed 'till I get this off to you!

I'm terribly sorry about all the trouble this has caused you, Ray! Believe me, Al and I have been so happy adapting your stories—not because we expect a sales increase, frankly, but simply because we love your stories and have been proud as hell that you've permitted us to "work with you!" The last thing we wanted was trouble for you!

So understand at the outset that, although you don't at present mind our continuing, don't hesitate at any time to request us to drop your stuff entirely if this condition you find yourself faced with continues, or in any way causes you further upset! O.K.?

Al Williamson, page 1 artwork for "A Sound of Thunder," from *Weird Science-Fantasy* No. 25 (Sept. 1954). (© William M. Gaines, Agent, Inc., 1953. Used with permission)

Jack Davis, page 1 artwork for "The Black Ferris," from *The Haunt of Fear* No. 18 (March–April 1953). Jack Davis stood over this original splash page in the summer of 1998 and shook his head in wonder. He remarked that his time with EC—especially his few adaptations of Ray Bradbury stories—provided some of his best moments in the comics industry. (© William M. Gaines, Agent, Inc., 1953. Used with permission)

Hell, we've been facing this same problem for many years—"comics," unfortunately, have a stigma attached which no amount of "quality" can overcome! But this is our problem, not yours, and I certainly don't want to see you dragged down, just as you're about to hit the top financially!

As to the practical aspects—cover plates have been made through the end of April! The last "horror" mag—Shock SuspenStories #9—is due to hit early in April, followed by the last issue with your name on the cover—Weird Science #20 near the end of April! I'd say that by the end of May, if not sooner, practically every copy with a cover blurb will be off the stands!

It's no trouble at all, Ray, so please think about it no more! Just a matter of your sweating out the next few months.

Now to bring you up to date! Lots of enclosures! First of all, a copy of Weird Fantasy *#18 (5 copies of which were shipped to you a week or so ago, and may already have arrived!) featuring "Zero Hour." Next, an advance copy of* Haunt of Fear *#18 with "Black Ferris"—the first of four issues to feature your picture and biography on the inside front cover! Howdaya like it? Hope you're pleased. More accurate figures on the circulation are as follows:*

Al Feldstein, original painting entitled *Space Arch*. This painting, a take-off of the *Weird Science-Fantasy* No. 24 cover, was originally done in 1954 as a private commission for Bill Gaines. It hung for years on Bill Gaines's office wall, just to the right of his desk chair, so it would always be within its owner's sight. Years later it was used as the cover for the third issue of the EC fanzine *Squa Tront*. (Painting © Al Feldstein, 1954)

HoF #18	450,000
WS #19	350,000
VoH #31	450,000
SS #9	400,000

1,650,000 total print with biography!

Next, five adaptations: "Touch and Go," "The Handler," "King of the Grey Spaces," "The Lake," and "The October Game"! I think every one of them is outstanding in one way or another, and I hope you enjoy 'em as much as we have! As usual, the boys worked their heads off—and I think it shows! (Congdon has been paid through these five—a total of 16!)

In the works are (#17) "The Changeling" and (#18) "I, Rocket"! I'm returning your photo, and tear sheets on "I, Rocket," as we're finished with them! (All other scripts and tear-sheets still safely and soundly locked away!)

Lastly, have enclosed a few representative letters! I don't send more because we're keeping "unused" letters for the present for use in future letter pages! Eventually you'll get all of 'em! (Ignore X's and marks—only our editing, etc.!)

Mail is divided into three classes:

"A" is friendly and favorable
"B" is confused but friendly
"C" mostly—they don't like you,
    Mr. B.!!!

Hope you get a kick out of them!
It's now 5:15 A.M.—so I's going to sleep! 'Night!!

                                    Bill

P.S. Special request: Please read "Judgment Day," last story in WF #18 (enclosed), an original by Al and myself—and give us your comment! It's causing a minor stir!!

To which Bradbury responded by February 3, 1953:

Al Feldstein, mid-1970s, photographed at his desk in the *Mad* offices. Photograph by E. B. Boater. (Courtesy of E. B. Boater. © E. B. Boater, 2002)

I can't say how much I appreciate your making such an easy matter out of an embarrassing situation. Your letter in reply to my decision to eliminate my name from your covers was a model of kindness and consideration I will never forget. Thanks so much. It is good to know you will help me out in this whole affair. . . .

Your offer to drop the adaptations at any time if I say so was certainly thoughtful also, but I see no reason to anticipate such an action; unless this snobbism rises to newer and sillier heights. I look forward to going ahead in the next year, enjoying myself thoroughly, seeing what you do with the adaptations.

I realize you have been battling the same battle, in the sea of comics, to try to do better things, and you have certainly succeeded with your s-f work, especially in such an item as your own JUDGMENT DAY which should be required reading for every man, woman, and child in the United States. You've done a splendid thing here, and deserve the highest commendation.

The adaptation proofs you sent on are on my desk now and I've been going over them. The work on TOUCH AND GO is quite amazing: I wondered how you would solve the various technical problems that inevitably would arise on a story of this sort. My best to Mr. Craig on this, and to Al. Ditto the work on THE HANDLER, THE OCTOBER GAME (which you handled well; it could have been terribly grisly; as it is, it is one of my unfavorite stories—I guess I'm getting old and sensitive, and now I have two wonderful girls, and this story now seems to be terribly depraved and frightening). THE LAKE was very nice. But I suppose my favorite this time, all around, is the work done by Severin and Elder on KING OF THE GREY SPACES; they have a very fresh technique, and the faces are unusually new and well-handled. I certainly hope you'll let them work on other of my stories, eh? I should think that would do well on something like THE ROCKET and THE MILLION YEAR PICNIC. . . .

Thanks for your understanding, your friendliness, and your help. I heard from Ted Dikty, one of the editors of the Best Science Fiction for each year, and he said: "I've recently had the opportunity to look over some of the publications issued by Educational Comics, containing adaptations of your stories, and was quite astonished at their quality. Their interpretation of your yarns was very intelligent and quite enjoyable."

Make you happy? I hope so.

What is so remarkable about this whole exchange of letters is that both author and publisher have genuine feelings and concerns about the other person's position. In the modern world where agents negotiate, authors are often driven solely by ego, and publishers either promise what they cannot deliver or never intend to deliver, these letters stand out as a beacon of decency. Bradbury himself was in a difficult position, and yet all he requested was help. Gaines may have felt some loss in not having the Bradbury name on his covers, but his ultimate concern was "What is best for Ray Bradbury's career?" Bradbury and Gaines belonged to a rare breed of man in a time when few would stand up for what they really believed in. Bradbury could have turned his back on the pulps, the comics, radio, or any other medium considered "inferior" to the world of letters; instead he actively engaged these other media and challenged the people working with him to produce their very best. It is no wonder then that EC's Ray Bradbury story adaptations now stand as masterpieces within their genre.

February 7, 1953

Dear Bill:

Thanks for yours of the 5th. As you know, I have enjoyed your adaptations so

Ray Bradbury, New York City, circa 1952–53. (Photo courtesy of the collection of Ray Bradbury. Used with permission. © Ray Bradbury, 2002)

much, or I wouldn't have written the letters, yet, as you yourself point out, my detractors can use these letters to point out how "Bradbury has fallen." Nothing we can do about such s.o.b.'s, except not give them a chance to pick up such convenient weapons.

It is a hellish and ambivalent situation. I am somewhat split on my relation to the literary world. I certainly would be a fool not to enjoy being called a top-writer in s.f., and yet I have seen what this sort of labeling can do to my other work. I know a woman who came up to me on the street not long ago, crying out, "Ray, Ray, why didn't you tell me!" "Tell you what?" I replied. "That you could write so well!" she cried. "I've put off reading your stories for so many years, because I thought they were science-fiction!"

So there you have it. One the one hand, being darned proud when you think of me in terms of being among the top ten in s-f today, and on the other being terribly afraid that my future books will not be read by Bernard DeVoto or Edmund Wilson, for instance, whose works I so much admire.

. . . Yes, by all means use my quote on JUDGMENT DAY. The story deserves to be praised by any thinking person. There are a lot of nasty little bigots around town I'd like to force this story on. . . .

> *All my best wishes, as ever,*
> *Ray*

Easter Sunday, 1953

Dear Bill:

It seems my letters must get shorter and shorter. So little time, so damn little . . . But at the risk of alienating all the hired artistic help, I must give the special nod this time out to Al Williamson for his delicate and sensitive evocation of I, ROCKET. A superb job. Thanks to him—And to Al, naturally!

I was delighted to hear you will use the two artists who worked on KING OF THE GREY SPACES on MILLION YEAR PICNIC. I look forward to this. . . .

July 18, 1953

Dear Bill:

The shortest note on record; in the throes of last days of rewriting THE FIRE MAN for Ballantine Books, to be published in October. Going mad correcting extrapolatory detail . . .

THE FLYING MACHINE is the finest single piece of art-drawing I've seen in the comics in years. Beautiful work; I was so touched and pleased by the concern for detail. . . .

Yours,
Ray

Thus ends the file of letters discovered during the 1970s. The correspondence gives readers an inside look at the constantly evolving relationship between Ray Bradbury and Bill Gaines during a time in American history when popular culture was under attack on every level. The novels of James Joyce were pulled from library shelves, the work of writers such as Jack Kerouac was declared "pornographic," the only available English-language edition of William Burroughs's *Naked Lunch* was a French paperback, and many authors discovered that their work could not be printed within the United States.

A February 1969 letter from Ray Bradbury to a young Jerry Weist, then publisher of the EC fanzine *Squa Tront*, sheds a bit more light on this era:

February 28, 1969

Dear Jerry:

Thanks for your good letter. Here is your comment.

My reactions to the appearance of my stories adapted for EC comics? Mixed.

The initial reaction, of course, one of great happiness. I had always wanted to have my own Sunday full-page panel. I still want it. But in the meantime, here was the chance to see my work done by some good illustrators and some fine illustrators.

The mixture of emotions, of course, came from the fact that I was beginning to get established in various other fields at the same moment. In 1953, when my name was appearing on more and more and yet more covers of EC magazines, my first films were beginning

Frank Frazetta, cover painting for *The Autumn People,* the first Ballantine paperback containing reprints of EC Bradbury stories. Ray Bradbury has stated upon many occasions that the "magic" of Frank Frazetta parallels the "magic" of his own stories. Emotional impact, intuition, and the ability to write or paint following one's creative instinct are the earmarks of genius shared by Frank Frazetta and Ray Bradbury. (Original paperback cover © Ballantine Books, 1965. Painting © Frank Frazetta estate, 2002. Used with permission)

to appear, and I was given the task of adapting into screenplay form the incredible MOBY DICK, directed by John Huston. I knew of the rampant snobbism in the world concerning comic strips of any sort. This was long before most of the intellectuals, if you can call them that, had latched onto admitting they read comics morning, noon, or night. Whereas my love was constant, beginning when I was 3 years old and sat on my dad's knee as he read HAPPY HOOLIGAN and the KATZENJAMMER KIDS to me. The love, which I suspect as being late and fraudulent, of the intellectuals, is a very recent thing. Only on occasion, over the years, have they expressed an interest in such strips as LI'L ABNER, 30 years ago, Barnaby in the '40's, and then in the 50's a strip like POGO. Most of the real attention has been paid in the past 5 or 6 years, and I say to hell with them. They wouldn't listen to us when it counted, so I won't let them into my club now. Their reasons for liking illustration and or comics are usually "made-up" anyway. They never relax. They don't know how to love from the inside out. They are always listening to each other from the outside in, which is a helluva way to love, which isn't love at all, but a gimcrack exercise, a substitute. They read critics to find out what is safe, what is "in." I never bothered to find out. I simply fell in love with BUCK ROGERS when I was 9 and collected him every day and every Sunday, and fell in love with TARZAN when I was 11 and collected him every day and every Sunday, and fell in love with PRINCE VALIANT when I was 17 or 18 and now have 32 years of VALIANT put away in my collection.

Anyway, to go on. I think that my favorite EC comics are the science-fictional ones. Not that I didn't enjoy the horror adaptations, I did, but it seems to me that the work Al Williamson did on I, ROCKET and THE ONE WHO WAITS is exceptional, as is the fine work of Wood on THERE WILL COME SOFT RAINS and MARS IS HEAVEN.

I also enjoyed the very clean work of Severin and Elder on KING OF THE GREY SPACES.

All the while I was happy with the above, I still lived in some faint fear of someone in the film complex where I was working speaking up and saying something like "Bradbury? Say, isn't he the guy who writes for those cheap comic books?"

I think we have all been through this time and time again, and have lived it out and finally found acceptance on many levels. Excellence is everywhere. On TV we find some of the finest work, ironically, occurring in the one minute commercials . . . both live-action and in cartoon or stop-motion animation. Similarly, in magazine commercial art, the best work is being done by advertising artists, not by gallery painters, in our country today. And nothing anyone

can say will change this truth. The galleries are almost empty of Ideas, and, need I add, customers. I didn't make the situation. I merely comment on it. At the very time we are most critical of materiality, art is being created in the midst of the dung heap. I find it vastly amusing. I find it reminiscent of Florence, Rome, and Venice, don't you, some few hundred years ago? When that hired "hack" Fra Angelico did "comic-strips" (have you ever seen them? look them up! in full color, oil) for the Church. Or the later hacks like Massacio, Da Vinci, or Michelangelo, all of them working for wages, eh?

Perhaps I reach too high, but the comparison is worth making. Our comic illustrators do NOT equal the work of the Fra Angelicos of that old world. But I make the comparison because I do want people to pay attention to the decent work, the good work, and occasionally the fine work that appears, only to vanish, day after day, Sunday after Sunday, in our lives.

I am indebted to the artists who illustrated my work for EC. I am happy to have their work collected in two books now by Ballantine. I no longer have to sneak around in the shadows with them, fearful of the criticism of the snobs. We have come out in the light, all of us. And the sun feels good, doesn't it, fellows?

THE END.

Again thanks, Jerry. Your SQUA TRONT is absolutely handsome. I particularly was happy to find the TIGA-Frazetta pages . . . very well done. I wish Frazetta could do more for all of us in the coming years. Enjoyed the Williamson portfolio and cover, also. My heartiest congratulations.

Ray Bradbury

This letter illustrates clearly that fifteen years after the last Bradbury science fiction story was published by EC, Bradbury had fond memories of the Feldstein adaptations.

During the period when the EC/Bradbury letters were originally written the author was working on *The Fireman*, which would become *Fahrenheit 451*, a novel about a future in which firemen burned books instead of putting out fires. It stands as a novel that speaks directly to the America of the 1950s, seen through the lens of a future time when men and women "became" the books that they feared would be burned.

AN INTERVIEW WITH AL FELDSTEIN, SEPTEMBER 13 AND 18, 2001
by Jerry Weist

Q: When and how did you first discover Ray Bradbury's work? Did you know of Bradbury before you became involved with EC Comics?

A: I read my first Ray Bradbury story after I'd been with EC for some time, and after we [Bill Gaines and I] had successfully launched our horror titles (based on our mutual love for the subject!). Bill and I were contemplating trying "science fiction" in comics (his suggestion, based on his love of the subject, one I knew nothing about!), and Ray Bradbury was part of my basic orientation into science fiction (along with John Campbell's *Astounding Science Fiction* magazine) the recommended reading by Bill Gaines to acquaint me with the genre. I was, to say the least, extremely moved by Ray Bradbury's distinctive style and the imaging in his prose.

Q: What was it about Bradbury's work that appealed to you?

A: After we were given permission to adapt Ray's stories into the comic book format for our science fiction titles, I obtained copies of *The Martian Chronicles, The Golden Apples of the Sun, The Illustrated Man,* and *The October Country*—all collections of Ray's stories—so that I could pick and choose the stories I wanted to adapt for our comic book titles. And it was while I was reading, analyzing, and adapting those stories that I became an avid and devoted Ray Bradbury fan. I felt that he was a "master artist" painting with descriptive words and lyrical syntax, masterful mind pictures. I marveled at his style, and I attempted with all of my comic book format know-how and experience to capture his inimitable storytelling talent into that form.

Q: Was there any direct communication between yourself and Ray Bradbury during the time that you adapted his stories for EC Comics?

A: Strangely, except for the four touching dedications and personal autographs that Ray did for me in my four collection volumes (when I sent them to him), I had little or no direct communication with him about the work. I have since learned, years later, that that communication was usurped by Bill Gaines . . . and that it was extensive. I had no idea at the time.

Q: Did both you and Bill Gaines work together to choose the stories to adapt, or was this selection left to you exclusively as editor for *Weird Fantasy, Weird Science,* and the other EC titles?

A: Bill was busy with other things, and it was I, as the editor and as the one doing the adaptations, who made all the decisions about which stories we would adapt and run. As it turned out, I fell so in love with his body of work that I adopted almost all of his stories available to me at the time, mostly [from] the four collections I cited above.

Q: How did you choose which Bradbury stories you would adapt?

A: Sheer emotional reaction, delight in their plot (if any) and in their mood and content . . . and the one overriding deciding factor: which EC artist I was adapting the story for! I would read story after story, some many times over again, looking for just the right one, both in subject matter and pictorial content, that would closely match the individual style and the individual ability of the specific EC artist whose next assignment I had to prepare and have ready. It was a marriage: story to artist and vice versa.

Q: Could you describe the time table allowed for these Bradbury adaptations? Did Bill Gaines give you more time, or any special guidelines to follow?

A: Each Bradbury story that I adapted was done in one day, as were all of the original stories I wrote for our various titles. That was the schedule. Four stories a week. One day reserved for editing or doing cover art. A "Bradbury Story Adaptation Day" was an evening-before off for Bill Gaines. He didn't have to come into the office the next morning with his usual "springboards"!

Q: The standard story page-count progression for every EC comic book title was 8-6-7-7 (i.e., the lead story was eight pages, the second story six pages, and the last two seven pages each). Few Bradbury story adaptations ended up with the eight-page count. Is there a reason for this?

A: We weren't confident enough that a Bradbury adaptation story would sit well with our readers as a "lead" story—the eight-pager. We were also concerned that his stories were sometimes just a little too "arty" for the "lead" eight-pager. So he was relegated to six- and seven-pagers, depending upon which artist was "up," and coming in for an assignment.

Q: Harvey Kurtzman was famous for drawing panel-by-panel, page-by-page guidelines for his artists to follow. Did you ever consider using this technique for the Bradbury adaptations, and how did your style as editor differ from the Kurtzman approach?

A: Throughout our association I had great respect for Harvey Kurtzman's creative and innovative talents. But the one thing that he did as an editor that I was vehemently opposed to was his desire to absolutely control the artists he wrote for by supplying them with his own personal graphic interpretations of the panels (in the form of tissue overlays), making each artist's finished product merely an extension of his own visual conceptions, thereby stifling the artist's own individual talent and imagination. I never considered doing that with my artists working on my stories for my titles. I used to liken myself (with my original stories) to the pastry chef who gives that "artist" chef a basic sponge cake, and allows him to decorate it with his own creative icing. And I continued that philosophy and that method of artist/editor collaboration with the Bradbury stories.

Q: Narrative (with plenty of narration text blocks) was a central component to almost every EC story in the 1950s. EC readers knew that a strong and developed narrative would be found in most EC stories. Did

this already-established format help or hinder your ability to adapt Bradbury short stories?

A: I'm not sure that the established EC format for original stories (at least, mine!) had anything to do with how I adapted a Bradbury story. His stories were uniquely and originally his. I made no attempt to instill my storytelling techniques into his story adaptations. That, I think, would have been sacrilegious—an insult to his vast talent—and sheer stupidity.

Q: The EC Ray Bradbury stories are now considered classics within the medium. Did you have any sense of this at the time, and why do you think these adaptations are still being reprinted and read today?

A: When I was doing them (and most of them I did with a tear or two brimming in my eyes because I was so moved!), I had the distinct feeling that our collaboration—Ray's original text my pictorial/text adaptation, and, of course, the marvelous artists'

William M. Gaines and Al Feldstein at the *MAD* offices, circa mid-1970s. Photograph by E. B. Boatner. (Courtesy of E. B. Boatner. © E. B. Boatner, 2002)

interpretations—was reaching a new level and cutting edge in the art of the comic book. When Ballantine Books reprinted the adaptations in their paperback book collections, I was delighted and flattered. [Ballantine Books reprinted sixteen of the EC stories in two paperbacks, *The Autumn People* and *Tomorrow Midnight,* printed in 1965 and 1966, respectively.]

Q: Bradbury, more than any other modern author, has had his stories adapted into almost every possible medium—from radio to TV to school plays. Why do you think that his work is so transferable? And why do so many (such as yourself) get the urge to adapt or transfer his work?

A: First of all, I do not necessarily agree that all of his work that has been transferred has been successfully transferred. Bradbury has to be read to be fully appreciated. You have to form those wonderful pictures in your mind that he paints with his wonderful words. Some dramatic adaptations of his writings (not those that were written explicitly for their medium!) have, in my opinion, failed to some extent. They lack the unique literary element of the original prose.

Q: To many people, Bradbury's stories seem to have an almost "timeless" quality. Can you comment on this?

A: Masterpiece art is "masterpiece art"! It shall prevail through all time! And the trash shall fall by the wayside and rot.

Q: Looking back at the 1950s through the lens of the year 2001, what memories or events stand out during your period of developing Bradbury adaptations for EC Comics?

A: The emotional delight, the immersion in a wonderful and exciting ongoing (for a few years, at least) creative endeavor, and the exciting and illuminating learning process that I experienced with the inevitable close study I made of each of his individual stories.

Promotional photograph of Bradbury with Barbara Rush, an actress in *It Came from Outer Space*, 1953. (© Universal Pictures Company, Inc., 1953)

Ray Bradbury hamming it up with a mock "Frankenstein" laboratory scene in the basement of the Los Angeles Film Society filming room, circa mid-1960s. (Photograph courtesy of the collection of Ray Bradbury. © Ray Bradbury, 2002)

CHAPTER 5

The Modern Renaissance Man: Bradbury on Radio and Television, and in the Movies

Photograph © Glynn Crain, 2001

Promotional photograph of Bradbury with Barbara Rush, an actress in *It Came from Outer Space,* 1953. (Image courtesy of the collection of Donn Albright. © Universal Pictures Company, Inc., 1953)

Stories abound of authors whose high-minded ideals and devotion to their craft are lost after exposure to the comparatively superficial values of Tinseltown.

Ray Bradbury's experience with Hollywood, however, was different. To begin with, he had grown up in Los Angeles and he later developed friendships with such diverse individuals as Charles Laughton, Rod Serling, Harlan Ellison, and Walt Disney. Further, Bradbury was a chameleon—his ability to adapt to various creative situations allowed him to outmaneuver or preempt potential failures. Time and again he refused to relinquish either his innocence or his enthusiasm, which enabled him to recoup his energies after "dancing the dance" with the army of individual and corporate interests that seem ever poised to crush true ingenuity in film.

And perhaps most important, Bradbury maintained a constant run of good luck when choosing collaborators. Was it fate that brought him to meet John Huston and co-write the screenplay for *Moby Dick*? If so, then fate led to an alchemy that transformed him. Was it luck or intuition that led Bradbury to suggest to François Truffaut that the director consider a new novel, just finished, about a future in which firemen burn books (rather than *The Martian Chronicles,* which Truffaut had initially wanted to film)? And *Icarus Montgolfier Wright,* the Academy Award–nominated short

TOP: Half-sheet poster for *It Came from Outer Space,* a movie made from Bradbury's screenplay *Atomic Monster,* 1953. (© Universal Pictures Co, Inc., 1953)

ABOVE: *It Came from Outer Space* cast posing as in poster, 1953. (Photograph courtesy of Photofest. © Universal Pictures Co, Inc., 1953)

RIGHT: Insert poster for *It Came from Outer Space,* 1953. (© Universal Pictures Co, Inc., 1953)

animated film based on Bradbury's short story, was an organic outgrowth of his previous relationship with artist Joseph Mugnaini.

Although later Bradbury was disappointed with the TV production of *The Martian Chronicles*, he soon moved on to assume control over the popular and successful *Ray Bradbury Theater*, which gave television viewers some of the purest and most direct adaptations of his short stories to date.

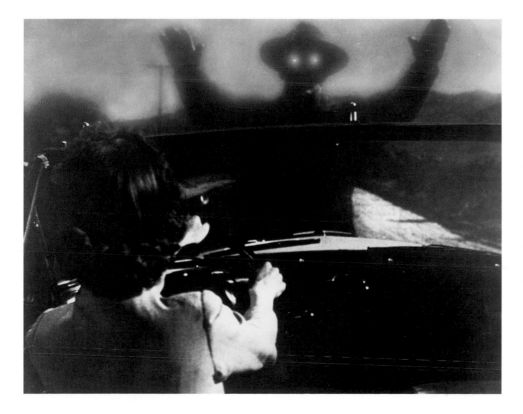

ABOVE LEFT: Window card posters for *It Came from Outer Space*, 1953. (Images courtesy of the collection of Forrest J Ackerman. © Universal Pictures Co, Inc., 1953)

TOP: The monster from *It Came from Outer Space*, 1953. (Photograph courtesy of the collection of Forrest J Ackerman. © Universal Pictures Co, Inc., 1953)

LEFT: Ellen (Barbara Rush) stops her car for Frank's alien double (Joe Sawyer) in *It Came from Outer Space*, 1953. (Image courtesy of the collection of Forrest J Ackerman. © Universal Pictures Co, Inc., 1953)

RIGHT: The monster from *The Beast from 20,000 Fathoms* (sometimes known as *Monster from Beneath the Sea*), 1953. This movie was based partly on the Bradbury story "The Fog Horn." Note the resemblance of the monster to a more famous Japanese one. (Photograph courtesy of the collection of Forrest J Ackerman. © Warner Bros., 1953)

ABOVE: A model of the monster used in the stop-motion animation for *The Beast from 20,000 Fathoms,* 1953. Bradbury later wrote a short story entitled "The Prehistoric Producer" about a dinosaur stop-motion animator. (Photograph courtesy of the collection of Forrest J Ackerman. © Warner Bros., 1953)

LEFT: Theater one-sheet poster for *The Beast from 20,000 Fathoms,* 1953. (Image courtesy of the collection of Ronald V. Borst. © Warner Bros. Pictures Distributing Corporation, 1953)

ABOVE AND INSET: Frederick Ledebur as Queequeg and Richard Baseheart as Ishmael in the
1956 *Moby Dick*. Bradbury shared screenplay
credit with director John Huston for this film.
Note Queequeg as an Illustrated Man precur
sor. (Photograph courtesy of Photofest, lobby
card courtesy of the collection of Ronald V.
Borst. © Warner Bros. Pictures Distributing
Corporation, 1956)

RIGHT: Bradbury with the body model used as a
tattoo guide for *The Illustrated Man*, 1968.
(Photo courtesy of the collection of Donn
Albright, used with permission. © Warner Bros.
Pictures Distributing Corporation, 1968)

Joseph Mugnaini, original paintings for *Icarus Montgolfier Wright*, 1962. Various scenes from the twenty-minute short animated film, based on a Ray Bradbury concept and co-written by Bradbury and George C. Johnson. The paintings are gouache and watercolor on illustration board. Joseph Mugnaini was the one artist that Bradbury felt closest to during his entire career. Mugnaini would illustrate books, do paintings for paperback covers, labor over lithographs that would be included in portfolios and limited-edition hardcover books, and eventually be drawn into the production of *Icarus Montgolfier Wright* during the early 1960s. These are the actual preliminary paintings used

in the short feature, on which the camera would focus in close-ups, pan in circular shots, and fade in and out from various angles. Mugnaini used color and his stark figurative painting style for the greatest emotional and expressive effects in this experimental animated work. The story relates the dream of man to fly, from the first mythic tale of Icarus to the hot-air balloon of Montgolfier and onward to the Wright brothers and the fire of the rocket ready to leap up to the stars in the final panel painting. (Paintings courtesy of Diana Robinson and the Joseph Mugnaini estate. © George C. Johnson/Joseph Mugnaini estate)

THE **BIG** ONES ARE COMING FROM UNIVERSAL!

Production has Started in London!

Winners of the 1965 New York Film Critics Award
BEST ACTRESS   **BEST ACTOR**

JULIE CHRISTIE   **OSKAR WERNER**

"**FAHRENHEIT 451**"

TECHNICOLOR®

Screenplay by   Based on the Novel by   Directed by   Executive Producer
FRANÇOIS TRUFFAUT and **JEAN-LOUIS RICHARD** · **RAY BRADBURY** · **FRANÇOIS TRUFFAUT** · **LEWIS M. ALLEN**
AN ANGLO-ENTERPRISE-VINEYARD FILMS PRODUCTION · A UNIVERSAL RELEASE

ABOVE: Promotional flyer announcing the start of production and release of *Fahrenheit 451*. (© Universal Pictures, 1966)

ABOVE RIGHT: Promotional photograph of Julie Christie for *Fahrenheit 451*, 1966. (Photograph courtesy of the collection of Ray Bradbury. © Universal Pictures, 1966)

CENTER RIGHT: *Cahiers du Cinéma in English*, No. 4. An English-translated version of the respected French film magazine *Cahiers du Cinéma* was briefly published in the 1960s. The inside back cover of this issue announces that the next issue will contain François Truffaut's diary on the filming of *Fahrenheit 451*. This diary was printed in two parts, in issues Nos. 5 and 6. (© Cahiers Publishing Company, 1966)

BELOW RIGHT: Promotional photograph of Oskar Werner and Julie Christie for Fahrenheit 451, 1966. (Photograph courtesy of the collection of Ray Bradbury. © Universal Pictures, 1966)

OVERLEAF: Original French 30" × 40" one-sheet poster for the movie *Fahrenheit 451*, 1966. (© Universal Pictures, 1966)

Lobby cards for the movie *Fahrenheit 451*, 1966. There were eight cards in total. (© Universal Pictures, 1966)

From "Truffaut on 'Fahrenheit 451,'" translated from the French by Kay Mander and R. K. Neilson Baxter, from *Cahiers du Cinéma in English*, No. 5.

JOURNAL OF "FAHRENHEIT 451," BY FRANÇOIS TRUFFAUT (PART ONE)

Monday 10 January 1966

Shooting on *Fahrenheit 451* was to have begun today, but it has been put off. The insurance company's doctor examined Julie Christie and found her too tired by her nine months' work on *Doctor Zhivago*.

Tuesday 11 January

. . . *Fahrenheit 451* is taken from a novel by Ray Bradbury. I read it at the end of 1960 and bought the rights in the middle of 1962. Why have I had to wait three and a half years before making it? Simply for money reasons. In my euphoria over *Jules and Jim,* I launched into a project that was financially too big for me. Responsible French producers who considered it decided it was too risky. I have to add that the adaptation we wrote, Jean-Louis Richard and I, never aroused much enthusiasm except among three or four of our pals.

Then it was the turn of the American companies. Again, reply negative. . . .

If the film gets made this time, it will be thanks to having Oskar Werner and Julie Christie in the cast. They have become big stars in the course of these last few months, and by pure coincidence both of them at this moment are receiving a shower of awards and Grands Prix and promises of Oscars.

In June 1963, a New York producer, Lewis Allen, bought the rights to *Fahrenheit* with the understanding that he would make it only with me. From that moment it became an English-language project, but yet it still took two years to find financial backing. . . .

Thursday 13 January

We begin this morning, without either Oskar or Julie, with scenes that will only be seen on various television screens in the film. . . .

Fahrenheit 451 is the super-simple story of a society in which it is forbidden to read and to possess books. The firemen—who once upon a time put out fire—are responsible for confiscating books and burning them on the spot. One of them, Montag, on the point of being promoted to a higher rank, influenced by meeting a young woman (Clarisse) who questions the order of things, begins to read books and to find pleasure in them. His own wife (Linda) informs on him out of fear, and eventually Montag is brought to the point of literally burning up his own captain. Then he runs away—and you will only need to buy a ticket to one of the better cinemas to find out where to.

. . . In point of fact, this film, like all those taken from a good book, half belongs to its author, Ray Bradbury. It is he who invented those book burnings that I'm going to have such fun filming, which is why I chose color. An old lady who chooses to be burned with her books rather than be separated from them, the hero of the film who roasts his captain, these are the things I am looking forward to filming and seeing on the screen, but which my imagination, tied too firmly to reality, could not have conceived by itself. After David Goodis and Henri-Pierre Roché, Ray Bradbury comes to my aid, providing me with the strong situations I need in order to escape from the documentary.

Sunday 16 January

A science fiction film makes everybody go creative, sometimes in the wrong way.

. . . Three years ago, the concept of *Fahrenheit 451* was an sf film, set in the future and backed up by inventions and gadgetry and so on. . . . Obviously it would be going too far to make *Fahrenheit 451* a period film, yet I am heading in that general direction. I am bringing back Griffith-era telephones, Carole Lombard–Debbie Reynolds–style dresses, a Mr. Deeds–type fire engine. I am trying for anti-gadgetry—at one point Linda gives Montag a superb cutthroat razor and throws the old battery-model Philips into the wastebasket. In short, I am working contrariwise, a little as if I were doing a "James Bond in the Middle Ages."

Wednesday 19 January

I have refused to authorize two writers to do a book about the making of the film. When they see this ship's log of mine they will probably think it is the reason for my refusal. This is not the case. In fact, it is because whenever I work from a novel, I feel a certain responsibility toward the author. Whether it comes off or not, whether it is faithful to the book or not, the film of *Fahrenheit 451* should only favor the sales of one book, the book from which it was taken. A book about the making of the film would only create confusion with Bradbury's. To my way of thinking, the best idea would be to reissue the novel, illustrating it with stills from the film.

Monday 24 January

The seven firemen go into the old lady's house. They spread out on the ground floor like a flock of migrating birds, and I suddenly realize that

Original French lobby cards for *Fahrenheit 451*, 1966. (© Universal Pictures, 1966)

Production and promotional photographs for *Fahrenheit 451*, 1966. Several of these and following photographs are those that Truffaut mailed to Bradbury. Montag (Oskar Werner) suits up. The firemen confront the old woman. The Captain (Cyril Cusack) and Montag in the old woman's secret attic library. (© Universal Pictures, 1966)

this scene is like *Johnny Guitar,* probably because of these men in black who have come to torment a woman who defies them from the top of her staircase.

What's more tiresome to film than seven men in one room? *Fahrenheit 451* is my fifth film and yet today I feel as if I am just a beginner. . . .

Tuesday 25 January

Seeing the firemen in her home, the old lady on the landing laughs and comes down the stairs, saying: "Play the man, Master Ridley, we shall this day light such a candle by God's grace as I trust shall never be put out." A little later in the story, through the mouth of the captain, Bradbury adds: "Words said by a man called Latimer to a man called Nicholas Ridley as they waited to be burned alive at Oxford on October sixteenth, 1555—for heresy."

. . . We will start the action of crane and flamethrower together and the flames will lick their way along a sheet of asbestos on the wall. . . .

Wednesday 26 January

I chose this woman to play the part of the old woman who burns with her books because she is small and round, a bit comical, to go against the convention of the dignified, valiant lady with the beautiful, ravaged face.

Thursday 27 January

In the attic library, a long monologue by the Captain about the usefulness of books. It's a difficult scene for Oskar Werner for he has to listen without answering back. Here I am again, with my usual problem of the antihero.

About a third of the way through the film, Montag reads a book but still continues to do his job normally and to go every day to the firehouse. He's in the position of the character in the Gestapo who would like to get interested in the Resistance without it really upsetting his life.

Tuesday 1 February

Hard day's work with the old lady surrounded by real flames, made by banks of gas jets hidden under the books. Six times in two hours she waved her arms and smiled before slumping down within a few feet of the gas jets. Her courage won everybody's admiration.

Wednesday 2 February

Full shot of the books on fire, then of the house burning. In the middle of the books, a dummy representing the woman . . . Obviously one take only. It works. The firemen ran out a little too quickly after the fire was lit, but Oskar bravely stepped forward again to pause in front of the fire before backing out of the house. . . .

Friday 4 February

Julie Christie is going to be wonderful, as easy to work with as Jeanne Moreau or Françoise Dorléac; like them, she's trusting, never fusses, and never asks theoretical questions like: "What is she feeling when she says so and so and this and that?"

Saturday 12 February

I have noticed only today that letting books fall out of frame doesn't work—I have to follow their fall right to the ground. In this film, books are characters, and to break into their flight is tantamount to leaving an actor's head out of the picture. I've felt from the start that several shots of this kind in the film didn't come off and now I know why.

Wednesday 16 February

. . . In the night, Montag gets out of bed and goes into the bathroom, where he takes a book out of its hiding place and sits down to read it in front of the television screen. It's really the first time he has ever read a book right from the beginning, so I got a lot of fun out of having him first decipher the title, then the name of the author, the publisher, the address of the printer, and so on, all with the laborious articulation of a child learning to read.

We have nearly finished with Julie as what my colleague Michelangelo Antonioni would call the "alienated" wife. Jean-Louis Richard and I did our best to make this part more sympathetic, more human than Bradbury's Mildred [*Note: Truffaut renamed Montag's wife "Linda" for his film; she was called "Mildred" in the book*], and Julie has made it more sympathetic still, particularly in contrast to Montag, who is overplaying the misogyny of the misunderstood husband. All this is becoming rather strange, subtler than the script, and more risky too.

Saturday 19 February

To the National Film Theatre with Helen Scott and Suzanne Schiffman—Renoir's *This Land Is Mine.* As the scenario of *Fahrenheit 451* was written with the Occupation and the Resistance constantly in mind, the two films have much in common. . . .

Two months ago, *Fahrenheit 451* as scripted was a tough, violent film, fine in its sentiments and rather serious. As shooting went on, I couldn't help feeling that I wanted to treat it more lightly; which led me to become more

Production and promotional photographs for *Fahrenheit 451*, 1966. The firemen search for books and throw them into a pile to be burned. Montag at home with wife and viewing the full-wall-screen TV. (© Universal Pictures, 1966)

Production and promotional photographs for *Fahrenheit 451*. Montag and the Captain burning the books discovered in Montag's house. (© Universal Pictures, 1966)

detached and to look to the future, as I looked to the past in *Jules and Jim,* with no pressure on the audience, no attempt to impose total belief in the concept. If I were to start the film again from scratch, I would say to the art director, the costume designer, the cameraman: "Let us make a film about life as children see it—the firemen are lead soldiers, the firehouse a super toy. . . ." I don't want *Fahrenheit 451* to look like a Yugoslav film or an American left-wing film. . . .

Sunday 20 February

We are embarking on the sixth week's work; we are almost halfway through the film and, as I have always done at this moment on my other films, I examine my conscience—which comes up with something like this: "You've been slapdash, you've been careless. You could have done better. Now you have the second half in front of you in which to pull up your socks, climb the slippery slope, and save the film."

JOURNAL OF "FAHRENHEIT 451," BY FRANÇOIS TRUFFAUT (PART TWO)

Tuesday 22 February

Continuation and end of the scenes in Clarisse's cellar. More trouble with Oskar Werner, who wanted to touch Clarisse's arm and shoulders, whereas I do not want any show of romance in their twosome. Again, after one of his lines he wanted Julie to look at him, which I didn't want.

Wednesday 23 February

. . . To tell the truth, *Fahrenheit 451,* which will disappoint the fantasy lovers, is science fiction in the style of *The Umbrellas of Cherbourg.* . . .

Monday 28 February

The opening scene of the film. In an apartment, a man gets up from the table to answer the telephone. All he hears is: "Hurry! . . . Quickly! . . . Get out now." He leaves on the run. This first man in the film, Jerry Spencer, we shall meet again at the very end with the bookmen.

Shortly after he leaves, the firemen arrive and search the apartment, finding books hidden in various places. . . .

Tuesday 1st March

. . . Ever since the script has been in existence I have had a preference for the role of Linda, conventional but moving, to that of Clarisse, which is the more seriously conventional because it is pseudo-poetical. People will say to me: "Why are you deliberately shooting two conventional roles?" My answer to that is that every film script has advantages and disadvantages, or rather that to make each point in the story involves the deliberate sacrifice of something. When one is navigating in the waters of science fiction, verisimilitude and psychology are not a serious matter if one makes up in plausibility and lyrical feeling what one loses by being out of tune with reality.

. . . So it is that I have de-sexed Clarisse so as to get neither her nor Montag mixed up in an adulterous situation which has no place in science fiction. . . .

Friday 4 March

These scenes of the fire engine going in and out of the firehouse seem to make everybody thoroughly childish, starting with the actors. It is sunny, it is warm, there is gaiety and good humor; in a word we enjoy ourselves.

From now on we are into the last third of the film, which means that the pattern of the jigsaw begins to show and that it becomes easier to fill in the gaps. . . .

By now, the mood and form of the whole film has become familiar to the whole unit. After three years of living with this story, it took me even three or four weeks shooting to find the pattern and another four weeks to see it accepted by everyone else. In the last analysis, it's a fairy tale, a fable, and an extravaganza, with nothing portentous about it at all.

Wednesday 9 March

The subjects of films influence the crews that make them. During *Jules and Jim* everybody started to play dominoes; during *La Peau Douce* everyone was deceiving his wife (or her husband); and right from the start of *Fahrenheit 451* everybody on the unit has begun to read. There are often hundreds of books on the set; each member of the unit chooses one and sometimes you can hear nothing but the sound of turning pages.

Friday 11 March

In my mind, and to fight against the conventional, Linda and Clarisse are two women who are almost identical, and I asked Julie not to play the two parts differently. For me, it was to be the same with Montag, who would have behaved gently and simply with both women. A man of the theater before everything, Oskar Werner could not accept that, and played for contrast. Having played Linda's husband violently, he wants to play the suitor to Clarisse, and doesn't realize the wrong he is doing to the

Production and promotional photographs for *Fahrenheit 451*. Montag burns the Captain. (© Universal Pictures, 1966)

characters; odious at home with his books, outside sweet and charming with his initiator.

In any case, he can't win the secret battle that has set us against one another, for in the editing I shall cut to Julie (either as Clarisse or Linda) each time it's necessary to get rid of too strong a gesture, too forced a smile, too grim a face.

Wednesday 16 March

Exterior of Montag's house. The first time he comes home, the time when he comes out and is shadowed by Clarisse, the time when Linda leaves the house to go and inform on him, the time when, as the fire engine pulls up, he cries: "But—this is my house!"

Friday 18 March

We continue to fit the jigsaw puzzle together. Clarisse and Montag in a scene which comes after the one in the school corridor. Rebuffed by the pupils, Clarisse, in the elevator, is weeping. Montag consoles her, and the scene ends with this line: "Do you remember what you asked me the other day . . . if I ever read the books I burn? . . . Last night I read one . . ."

. . . In Montag's apartment, I did a shot of Oskar reading the beginning of *David Copperfield.* It was an over-shoulder shot and one could see the page but not closely enough to read the words. So we took closer and closer shots on the opening page with its chapter heading, "I am born."

Saturday 19 March

. . . I like Cyril Cusack's performance and his voice very much. Gentleness, kindness, and modesty are qualities that come over on the screen, and the role of the Captain has gained in humanity on consequence. Obviously, Montag now looks like a heel rather than a hero when he burns him up, but as I don't like heroes, all is well.

Thursday 24 March

. . . We filmed, camera on the ground, the evolutions of the little red helicopter which has to come down very low over the roof of the firehouse, so that in the same shot we can cover the death of the "substitute Montag," struck down by a burst of machine-gun fire from the helicopter. According to the script, this scene should have taken place in a cul-de-sac, but the production not having enough cash left to build three bits of blank wall, I transposed all of it to the exterior of the firehouse, a setting which emphasizes the callous fiendishness of the authorities who, in order to stage Montag's death convincingly, sacrifice the life of another man.

Production and promotional photographs for *Fahrenheit 451.* Prior to torching his boss, Montag learns to read. Montag and Clarisse share a tender moment. Montag with Clarisse (Julie Christie) destroying the forbidden papers she's found in her uncle's possession. Final scene: Montag and Clarisse in the snowy rail-yard of the bookmen. (© Universal Pictures, 1966)

All of this will be shown on a TV set in the derelict old railway coach used by the bookmen, in the presence of Montag himself, who will thus witness his own capture and execution. If I've not made this very clear, you can always hope that the film will make it clearer.

Friday 25 March

. . . Actually what dominated the day was the euphoria of the whole unit at the prospect of going to France. We are leaving for the evening for Chateauneuf-sur-Loire, near Orléans, to do three scenes with an elevated monorail out in the country, which I spotted as long ago as 1962 when the film was going to be made in France. This monorail, which is where Clarisse and Montag first meet, serves as the link between the firehouse and Montag's home. Although already outdated by its air-cushion rival, it's the only vaguely futuristic element in the film and that is why I have never wanted to give it up. . . .

Sunday 27 March

I pick up Nick Roeg in Paris and we drive to Orléans.

. . . Thirty or forty lines each evening are like a daily letter addressed to Jean-Pierre Léaud, Godard, de Givray, Aurel, Rivette, Jean-Louis Richard, and, naturally, Bradbury, who is intrigued to the point where, for the first time in his life, he bought an airline ticket with the intention of coming to see us. At the last moment his aerophobia triumphed and he gave the expedition up, but as consolation we sent him fifty stills from the film *"fortement legendées"* [lavishly captioned] as they say in the editorial room of *Cahiers,* or is it the magazine *Lui?* I can no longer remember.

Friday 1st April

At Black Park, close to Pinewood, we tackle the final scene of the film, the one with the book-men.

Saturday 3 April

. . . I thought of an idea that would have worked well in *Fahrenheit 451* but which I shan't carry out, having lost my interest in Oskar Werner. Montag in the course of a nocturnal reading session would discover a book with uncut pages. Wanting to read it, he would not be able to turn them because they would appear to be stuck together; in short, he would not understand this mysterious object at all. . . .

Production photographs for *Fahrenheit 451.* François Truffaut with Julie Christie. The old woman, Julie Christie, and the old woman's stunt double pose for a special photograph. Bottom photograph by Norman Horgood. (Photographs courtesy of the collection of Ray Bradbury. © Universal Pictures, 1966)

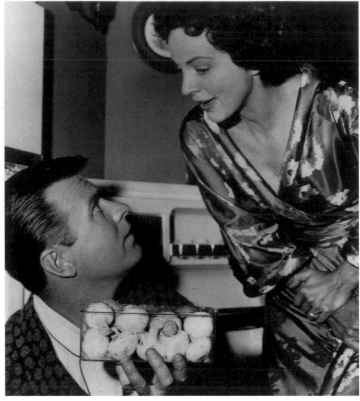

ABOVE LEFT: Alfred Hitchcock on *Alfred Hitchcock Presents*. This show ran from 1955 to 1962, after which it was expanded to an hour and renamed *The Alfred Hitchcock Hour*. (Photograph courtesy of Photofest. © *Alfred Hitchcock Presents* CBS, 1959)

ABOVE RIGHT: *Alfred Hitchcock Presents*, "Special Delivery," starring Steve Dunn and Beatrice Straight (CBS), telecast on November 29, 1959. Bradbury wrote the teleplay, based on his short story "Come into My Cellar." (Photo courtesy of Photofest. © *Alfred Hitchcock Presents*/CBS, 1959)

LEFT: Electric grandmother (Josephine Hutchinson) with children (left to right: Veronica Cartwright, Dana Dillaway, Charles Herbert), from *The Twilight Zone*, "I Sing The Body Electric!" (CBS), telecast on May 18, 1962. Bradbury wrote the teleplay, which he later developed into a short story. (Photo courtesy of Photofest. © *The Twilight Zone*/CBS, 1962)

JOURNAL OF "FAHRENHEIT 451," BY FRANÇOIS TRUFFAUT (PART THREE)

Tuesday 12 April

. . . Several bookmen introduce themselves to Montag, always in the same way, giving the name of the book and its author. Example: "I am *The Pickwick Papers*, by Charles Dickens." For Jane Austin's *Pride and Prejudice* I chose twins. When Montag asks: "Both of you the same book?", they reply: "My brother's Volume One—My brother's Volume Two." The choice of this book will give the knowing critics a bone to pick. They will take great pleasure in pointing out that *Pride and Prejudice* has never been published in two volumes.

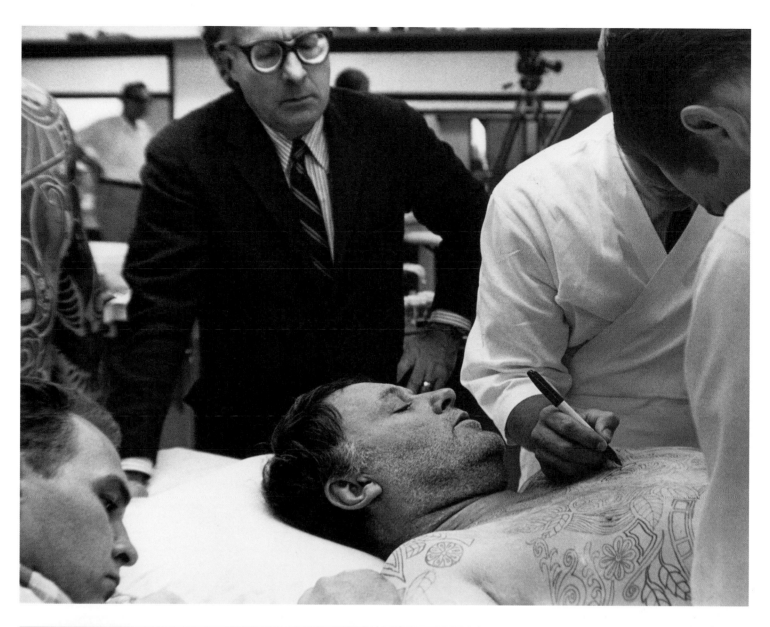

In the film, Henri Brulard adds for Montag's benefit: "We call the first Pride and the other Prejudice." It's not all that subtle but I feel that if we don't have a few jokes among the bookmen, we shall wind up with a truly frightful solemnity.

Thursday 14 April

This morning at six o'clock, from my window on the twenty-fifth floor of the Hilton, I watched the snow fall over all of London, thick, packed, unyielding. Black Park has become White Park!

I decided to shoot just the same and to make a virtue out of the snow. We laid a floor of rostrum-tops over the swamp ground at the head of the lake, put campfires in one or two places down the shores, and by midday we were ready to turn the camera on the long final shot. . . .

Wednesday 20 April

. . . Ray Bradbury gave me a free hand in adapting his novel, for he knew it would be difficult, having tried himself to make a stage play from it. Jean-Louis Richard and I worked on the construction for ten or twelve weeks, and having finished the job at the beginning of 1963, we have often taken it up again since, tightened it, reshaped it, so as to keep the story down to 110 minutes and keep the budget down.

It will surely be an offbeat film, especially for an English-language production, but within its strangeness it seems to me to be coherent.

. . . Come to think of it, is Proust burning in *Fahrenheit 451?* No, but this omission will soon be corrected.

Thursday 28 April

. . . This time it is really the last day of shooting.

Friday 29 April

For the first time, uninterrupted screening of the complete film . . . There are, in fact, two endings—the time where Montag burns up the Captain. Then a vague manhunt begins, vague because it isn't menacing enough, and tacked on after this phony chase is the sequence with the bookmen. This has the merit of bringing the chase sequence to a neat ending, by the conclusive faked execution shown on the TV set in the bookmen's railway coach.

Tuesday 10 May

I had thought to bring this diary to an end on the last day of shooting, but Jean-Louis Comolli has asked me to try and carry it on until the editing. . . .

The original model used to paint the tattoos for *The Illustrated Man*. This model was used each day when the special-effects artists applied the tattoos to the body of actor Rod Steiger. (© Warner Bros.–Seven Arts, 1968)

Wednesday 18 May

We are going to try to replace the usual fade-outs to black by fade-outs to white. This will have a more science fiction effect, but the trouble will be that after a few screenings in the cinemas the inevitable scratches will show up much more on the white. . . .

Friday 20 May

In the mail a letter from Ray Bradbury. He is delighted that the film ends up in the snow. He has himself adapted his *Martian Chronicles* and is sending me a copy of the script.

Thursday 26 May

The music is important and there will be a lot of it, but Bernard Herrmann and I have agreed that it should not be in itself significant. If *Fahrenheit 451* is a flop commercially it won't be the music that will make it any less of a flop. So all it has to do is to parallel the strangeness of the scenes. . . . From the very start of our discussion we rejected electronic effects or *musique concrète* and, in general, all the commonplace and futuristic clichés in to which television, be it in the USA or Europe, falls headfirst.

Thursday 2 June

Jean Aurel has agreed to take time off from other commitments to hop across to London and look at *Fahrenheit 451.* He is an expert on the construction of films and, like Jacques Becker, with whom he collaborated, a fanatic about visual clarity. . . . He arrived, looked at the film, took some notes in the dark, and then we talked. He likes it and reminds me that he was always afraid that the story, or rather the theme of the film, had always scared him as being very indigestible. He considers that I have been out on a limb, certifies that the story works, and is particularly complimentary about all the parts played by the books—books read, books stolen, hidden, burned, that is to say my whole reason for wanting to make the film. He has one big criticism, at once

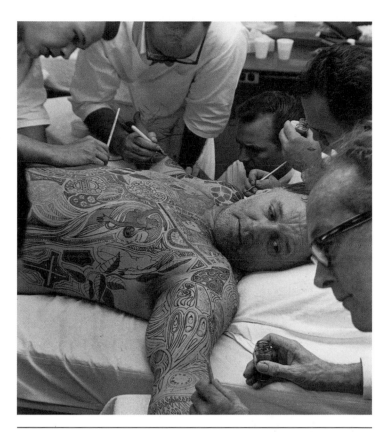

Makeup director Gordon Bau and a team of eight assistants spent ten hours applying the temporary tattoos to Rod Steiger's torso. An additional full day was needed to "tattoo" his hands, legs, and lower body. (Photo courtesy of Photofest. © Warner Bros.–Seven Arts, 1968)

Rod Steiger in the movie *The Illustrated Man.* (Photograph courtesy of the collection of Forrest J Ackerman. © Warner Bros. Seven Arts, 1968)

What would you
give a man
who could
make your
deepest dream
come true?

Ray Bradbury's

Something Wicked This Way Comes

RAY BRADBURY'S "SOMETHING WICKED THIS WAY COMES"
A JACK CLAYTON FILM Starring JASON ROBARDS JONATHAN PRYCE
DIANE LADD PAM GRIER Produced by PETER VINCENT DOUGLAS
Screenplay by RAY BRADBURY Based on his Novel Directed by JACK CLAYTON
Music Composed by JAMES HORNER TECHNICOLOR ® ▢▢ DOLBY STEREO
From WALT DISNEY PRODUCTIONS [Read the Bantam Book]
Lenses and Panaflex Camera by PANAVISION ® PG PARENTAL GUIDANCE SUGGESTED
Released by BUENA VISTA DISTRIBUTION CO., INC © 1983 Walt Disney Productions   SOME MATERIAL MAY NOT BE SUITABLE FOR CHILDREN

ABOVE: Poster for the movie *Something Wicked This Way Comes,* based on the book by Ray Bradbury. Bradbury also wrote the movie's screenplay. (© Walt Disney Productions, 1983)

LEFT: Publicity photographs for *Something Wicked This Way Comes.* Lighting rod salesman Tom Fury (Royal Dano) discovers a woman encased in ice. Jason Robards as librarian Charles Halloway. (© Walt Disney Productions, 1983)

serious and yet unformed: for him the film gets under way rather late—only when Montag reads a book for the first time at the end of the fourth reel. . . .

Next morning, I again ran the first four reels for him, and he found a solution in the cutting continuity which I adopted at once, so obvious did it seem. It's a matter of transposing two long scenes, thus introducing Clarisse before Linda. It so happens that by doing this we go back to the construction of the novel which I had thought it was necessary to modify. Hurrah for Bradbury! . . .

Friday 10 June

Arrival of Luigi Chiari, who came and viewed the film. The second "fresh look" after Jean Aurel. He has accepted the film for the Venice Festival and has

TOP: Bradbury with cast of *Something Wicked This Way Comes,* 1983. (Photograph courtesy of the collection of Ray Bradbury. © Walt Disney Productions, 1983)

ABOVE: Lobby cards for *Something Wicked This Way Comes.* Mr. Dark (Jonathan Pryce), Will, and Jim (Vidal I. Peterson and Shawn Carson), and the Dust Witch (Pam Grier). (© Walt Disney Productions, 1983)

himself set the date of the showing, the seventh of September. So now we must make haste to "spot" the dialogue of the film, in order to work out the French and Italian subtitles. I have never been so happy to have a film invited to a festival as this time, doubtless because of my feeling of isolation in the course of all this work away from Paris. . . .

Monday 13 June

I hope no one will read any deliberate meaning into the choice of books featured in *Fahrenheit 451*. . . .

. . . Quite deliberately, personal choice had little to do with it. The point was to film the books as *objects*.

Tuesday 21 June

Although the adaptation of *Fahrenheit 451* was written a year before the screenplay of *La Peau Douce,* there are, strangely enough, a number of things common to both films, and if Montag's wife is called Linda—and not Mildred as in Bradbury's book—it's probably because the Jacoud affair was already in my mind. For the rest, *Fahrenheit 451* will probably be more like *Shoot the Piano Player*, perhaps because in both cases we are dealing with an American novel, stocked with American material.

I don't know what the film will look like; I know it will look only remotely like what I have written about it here since, quite obviously, I shall have spoken only of what was unexpected or impressed me, and not of what was accepted long ago either in my mind or in Bradbury's. Now, on the screen you will see only what was in our two heads, Bradbury's brand of lunacy and then mine, and whether they have blended together well.

My films, like those of a lot of filmmakers, are conceived from the idea of a blend, from the desire to take "the mixture as before" and blend the ingredients together in fresh quantities: "Listen, wouldn't it be interesting to tell that kind of story but to treat it in a different way from the usual one?" Here, in the case of *Fahrenheit 451,* it was a case of treating a fantasy with familiarity, making out-of-the-ordinary scenes look ordinary and everyday scenes look abnormal. I still don't know whether the result will give the impression of a sane film made by a madman or a mad film made by a sane man, but I am convinced that when we write a book or make a film we are abnormal beings holding forth to normal people. Sometimes our madness is accepted, sometimes it is rejected. Ever since I came to understand this, the question of knowing whether one or another of my films would be a success or not worried me less and less, and I shall never again experience the fear I had when I was making *The Four Hundred Blows*—that no one would be in the least interested.

The Illustrated Steiger. The second major film to be made from a Bradbury book was *The Illustrated Man.* Starring Rod Steiger and Claire Bloom, this complicated movie attempted to knit together three of the more important stories from the book. Steiger would endure one of the most time-consuming and difficult makeup jobs in Hollywood history—some days he spent well over ten hours under the lights with the special-effects crew, who had to repaint his body for each new day of filming.

ROCK HUDSON in Ray Bradbury's "THE MARTIAN CHRONICLES"

ROCK HUDSON in Ray Bradbury's "THE MARTIAN CHRONICLES"

TOP: *Television Times* (Jan. 27–Feb. 2, 1980), special issue highlighting the NBC-TV miniseries broadcast of *The Martian Chronicles* on January 27, 28, and 29, 1980. (Image courtesy of the collection of Donn Albright. © Television Times Inc., 1980)

ABOVE AND LEFT: Publicity photographs from *The Martian Chronicles.* (© Charles Fries Productions, Inc., 1979/NBC, 1980)

ABOVE: Cover of shooting script no. 2 for *The Martian Chronicles,* scripted by Richard Matheson, cover art by Doug Wildey. (© NBC, 1980)

RIGHT AND ABOVE RIGHT: Publicity photographs for *The Martian Chronicles.* Martians in two different scenes. (© Charles Fries Productions, Inc., 1979/NBC, 1980)

COMING IN JULY FROM BUENA VISTA HOME VIDEO

THE RAY BRADBURY THEATER

THE CROWD

© MCMLXXXV Atlantis Films Limited.

Your host: Master storyteller Ray Bradbury

© MCMLXXXV Atlantis Films Limited. © MCMLXXXIII Buena Vista Distribution Co., Inc.

Permission is hereby granted to newspapers and magazines to reproduce these photographs on condition that they are accompanied by their respective copyright notices.

ABOVE LEFT: Promotional flyer for the video of *The Ray Bradbury Theater* episode "The Crowd." This episode (the third) aired July 2, 1985. *The Ray Bradbury Theater* was on television from 1985 to 1992, sixty-five episodes in all. It was first produced by HBO, and later by USA Productions. It featured Bradbury as the host, and episodes were based on Bradbury stories with teleplays written by Bradbury. It was quite popular in France. Actors such as William Shatner, Drew Barrymore, Peter O'Toole, and Jeff Goldblum appeared in episodes. (© Atlanta Films Limited, 1985/Buena Vista Distribution Co., Inc., 1983)

ABOVE RIGHT: *The Ray Bradbury Theater,* "And the Moon Be Still As Bright." This episode (the thirty-seventh) aired October 19, 1990. (Photograph courtesy of Photofest. © *The Ray Bradbury Theater*/USA, 1990)

CENTER LEFT: Sally Kirkland as the mother in *The Ray Bradbury Theater* production of "Zero Hour." This episode (the forty-fourth) aired January 10, 1992. (Photograph courtesy of Photofest. © *The Ray Bradbury Theater*/USA, 1992)

BOTTOM LEFT: *The Ray Bradbury Theater,* "The Day It Rained Forever." This episode (the fortieth) aired November 9, 1990. (Photograph courtesy of Photofest. © *The Ray Bradbury Theater*/USA, 1990)

ABOVE: *The Ray Bradbury Theater,* "The Utterly Perfect Murder." This episode (the forty-eighth) aired February 7, 1992. (Photograph courtesy of Photofest. © *The Ray Bradbury Theater*/USA, 1992)

RIGHT: David Carradine in *The Ray Bradbury Theater* production of "And the Moon Be Still as Bright." This episode (the thirty-seventh) aired October 19, 1990. (Photograph courtesy of Photofest. © *The Ray Bradbury Theater*/USA, 1990)

FAR RIGHT: *The Ray Bradbury Theater,* "The Jar." This episode (the forty-fifth) aired January 17, 1992. (Photograph courtesy of Photofest. © *The Ray Bradbury Theater*/USA, 1992)

Ray Bradbury, circa 1960, in the Los Angeles Film Society basement film room, sitting in the original "time machine" prop from the 1960 film version of H. G. Wells's *The Time Machine*. (Photograph courtesy of the collection of Ray Bradbury. © Ray Bradbury, 2001)

LEFT: Flyer and photographs from *The Martian Chronicles,* stage production of the University of Texas Theatre for Youth, circa 1980s. (© Ray Bradbury, 2002)

BOTTOM LEFT: *The Martian Chronicles,* from the Ray Bradbury Festival, Manasqua High School, Manasqua, N.J., November 1995. (© Ray Bradbury, 2002)

BELOW: Program from the Ray Bradbury Festival, Manasqua High School, Manasqua, N.J., November 1995. Photograph: Lee Weisert, director, and Jeffrey Eirich, assistant director. (© Ray Bradbury, 2002)

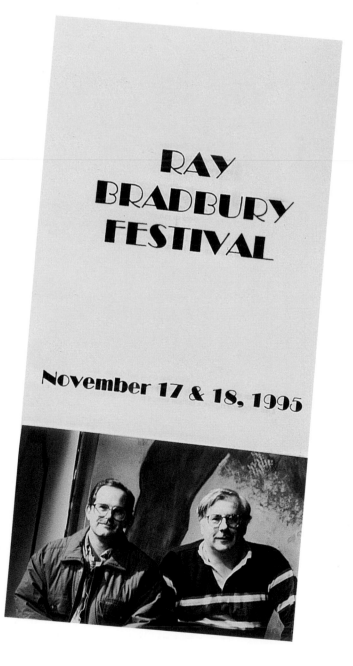

RAY BRADBURY FESTIVAL

November 17 & 18, 1995

The Theater and Ray Bradbury: From Private Passions to Public Performances

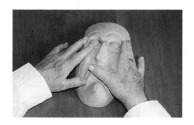

Photograph © Glynn Crain, 2001

BOTTOM LEFT AND RIGHT: *The Martian Chronicles,* from the Ray Bradbury Festival, Manasqua High School, Manasqua, N.J., November 1995. (© Ray Bradbury, 2002)

Ray Bradbury's lifelong love affair with the theater began in his youth. Years later, time and again high school–age theater groups requested permission to adapt his stories for local stage performances. Bradbury has never been a cultural snob, and he acquiesced to almost every early request. Then one day he said to himself, "If high school kids can do it, then so can I!"

As he now gladly admits, the genie was immediately and forever out of the bottle. Today, at eighty-two, Ray Bradbury takes great joy in attending performances of plays he has authored, many of them at the Colony Theatre in Los Angeles. Terrence Shank—director, stage designer, and producer at the Colony—has become Bradbury's "partner in wonder." Under Shank's leadership (1975 to 1984), the Colony was honored with sixteen Los Angeles Drama Critics Circle nominations, ten Awards for Distinguished Achievement, and a Special Award for Continuing Excellence in Production. In 2000, Shank rejoined old friends to collaborate on a revival of Bradbury's *Dandelion Wine* at the Colony's new theater in Burbank.

ABOVE: Bradbury at the Orpheum Theatre, New York City, 1965. (Photograph courtesy of the collection of Donn Albright. © Ray Bradbury, 2002)

RIGHT: Poster for the world premiere of *The World of Ray Bradbury,* Coronet Theatre, Pandemonium Theatre Company, Los Angeles, 1964. Poster graphics by Joseph Mugnaini. (© Pandemonium Theatre Company, 1964)

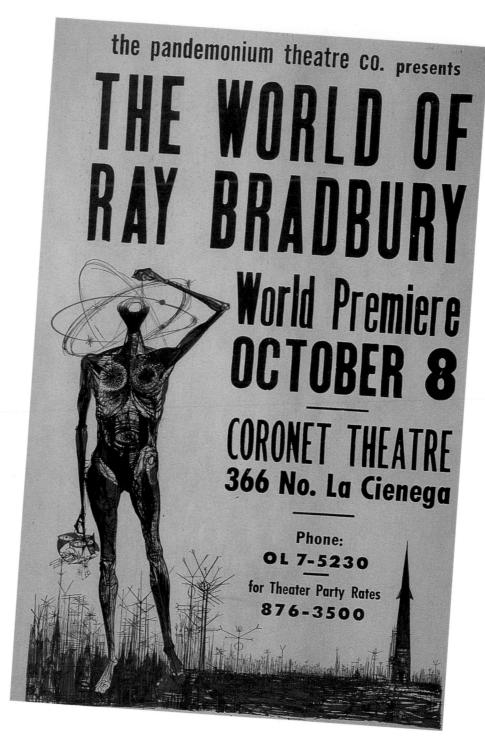

Bradbury's good friend the great American actor Charles Laughton shared his wisdom and insight about stagecraft with him; Bradbury credits Laughton with teaching him how to "stay with the character," and how to speak directly to the audience through a central character. While many people might assume that writing a play is not much different than writing a book or short story, Bradbury acknowledges that each form has its unique set of challenges—and rewards.

ABOVE: Bradbury with a theater group, just before a performance. (© Ray Bradbury, 2002)

RIGHT: Original theater poster for *Leviathan '99,* using Joseph Mugnaini's painting for *S Is for Space. Leviathan '99* is a space-age drama by Ray Bradbury, and was presented at the Samuel Goldwyn Studios Stage Nine Theatre. (© Samuel Goldwyn Studios, 1976)

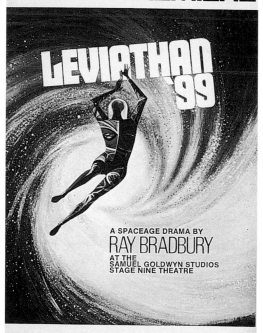

THE CRICKET THEATRE PRESENTS

THE MARTIAN CHRONICLES

April 28 - May 23 - '76

A WORLD PREMIERE!

by Ray Bradbury   directed by Howard Dallin
Adults $4.00 Students $2.75   MAT Vouchers Accepted
FOR RESERVATIONS CALL 333-1411   THE CRICKET THEATRE 13th & Univ. Aves. N.E.

RIGHT: Original theater poster for *The Martian Chronicles,* Cricket Theatre, Minneapolis, Minn., 1976. (© Cricket Theatre, 1976)

LEFT: Original theater poster for *Something Wicked This Way Comes,* Northern Light Theatre. (© Northern Light Theatre Productions)

BELOW: Original theater poster for *Dandelion Wine,* artwork by Barber. Arena Stage, adapted by Peter John Bailey. (© Arena Stage Productions, 2002)

RAY BRADBURY'S

Something Wicked This Way Comes

THEATRE BALLET

GYLLIAN RABY/Adapter and Director   DAVID RIMMER/Composer   LAMBROS LAMBROU/Choreographer

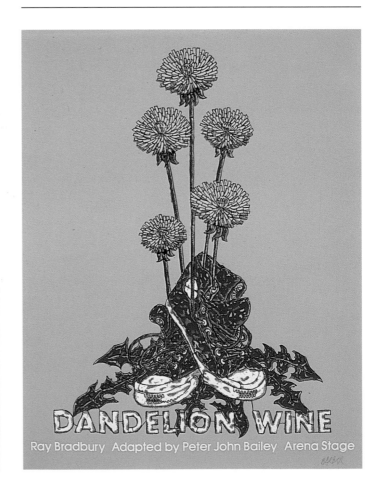

DANDELION WINE

Ray Bradbury Adapted by Peter John Bailey Arena Stage

LEFT: Promotional sheet for *Something Wicked This Way Comes,* Northern Light Theatre. (© Northern Light Theatre Production)

RIGHT: Photograph of Ray Bradbury at recent performance, Forry Ackerman and Anne Hardin stand in the background. (© Ray Bradbury, 2001)

Backstage at the Colony Theatre's 1977 production of *The Martian Chronicles*. (© The Colony Theatre Company, 2002)

A scene from the Colony Theatre's 1977 production of *The Martian Chronicles*. (© The Colony Theatre Company, 2002)

"The Third Landing," a scene from the Colony Theatre's 1977 production of *The Martian Chronicles.* Note backdrop by Joseph Mugnaini. (© The Colony Theatre Company, 2002)

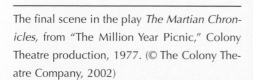

The final scene in the play *The Martian Chronicles,* from "The Million Year Picnic," Colony Theatre production, 1977. (© The Colony Theatre Company, 2002)

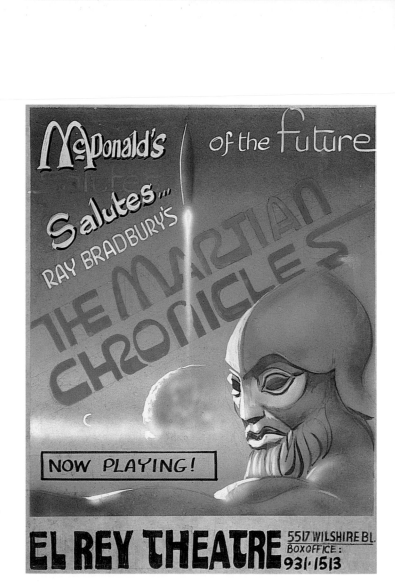

RIGHT: Ray Bradbury with two Martians and director Michael David Wadler, during a run of the new version of *The World of Ray Bradbury,* which premiered at the Colony Theatre in 1995. (Photograph by Bob Lapin, courtesy of the Colony Theatre. © The Colony Theatre Company, 2002)

LEFT: A scene from "The First Landing," in *The Martian Chronicles* at the Colony Theatre in 1977. James Howard Davis as Yll and Dess Croxton as Ylla. (Photograph by David Talbert, courtesy of the Colony Theatre. © The Colony Theatre Company, 2002)

RIGHT: From *Dandelion Wine* at the Colony Theatre in 1981. John Allee as Douglas Spaulding, Todd Nielsen as Bill Forrester, Theresa Bailey as Tarot Witch. (Photograph by David Talbert, courtesy of the Colony Theatre. © The Colony Theatre Company, 2002)

BELOW: Harold Gould in *To the Chicago Abyss* at the Colony Theatre, 1995. Note the Mugnaini projected-cel background. (© the Colony Theatre Company, 2002)

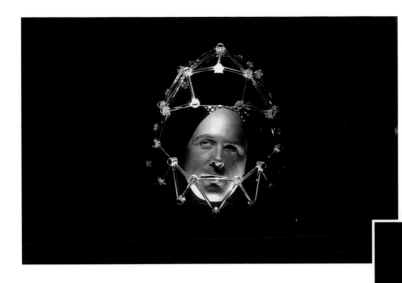

ABOVE AND RIGHT: From *The World of Ray Bradbury: Kaleidoscope* at the Colony Theatre in 1995. Steve Gustafsen and Melissa Hanson. (Photograph by Bob Lapin, courtesy of the Colony Theatre. © The Colony Theatre Company, 2002)

LEFT: From *The World of Ray Bradbury: Pillar of Fire* at the Colony Theatre in 1995. Jacy Crawford as Lantry. (Photograph by Bob Lapin, courtesy of the Colony Theatre. © The Colony Theatre Company, 2002)

RIGHT: From *The World of Ray Bradbury: To the Chicago Abyss* at the Colony Theatre in 1995. Lon Huber, Laura Wernette, Bean Morocco. (Photograph by Bob Lapin, courtesy of the Colony Theatre, © The Colony Theatre Company, 2002)

Joseph Mugnaini, original artwork for production "cel" background. These colored gel cels were projected onto stage backdrops for dramatic effect during Colony Theatre performances of Bradbury plays. (Images courtesy of the collection of Ray Bradbury. © Joseph Mugnaini estate, 2002)

LEFT: Harold Gould in *To the Chicago Abyss* at the Colony Theatre, 1965. Note Mugnaini projected-cel background. (© The Colony Theatre Company, 2002)

BELOW: Joseph Mugnaini, original artwork for production cel backgrounds. The top two are matching landscapes for *The Pedestrian;* the bottom two are matching interior scenes for *To the Chicago Abyss.* (© Joseph Mugnaini estate, 2002)

LEFT: Dennis Patrick and Harold Gould in the Colony Theatre's 1965 production of *The Pedestrian*. Note the projected background artwork by Joseph Mugnaini. (© The Colony Theatre Company, 1965)

BELOW: Joseph Mugnaini, original artwork for production cel backdrops for *The Pedestrian* at the Colony Theatre. Mugnaini's use of futuristic architectural forms was perfect for this theater adaptation of Bradbury's story. (Images courtesy of the collection of Ray Bradbury. © Joseph Mugnaini estate, 2002)

LEFT: Preliminary sketch by Joseph Mugnaini of "rocket gantry" backdrop for the play *Leviathan '99*, watercolor on paper. Bradbury gave this original sketch to Forrest J Ackerman at Christmas, 1975. (© Joseph Mugnaini estate, 2002)

BELOW: Joseph Mugnaini, original artwork for background cel for *The Wonderful Ice Cream Suit*. (© Joseph Mugnaini estate, 2002)

Joseph Mugnaini, original cel backgrounds for scenes from various Ray Bradbury plays at the Colony Theatre. (© Joseph Mugnaini estate, 2002)

EXCERPT FROM THE THEATER PRODUCTION OF FAHRENHEIT 451

The following scene from the theater production of *Fahrenheit 451* has never seen print until now. It is an important exchange between Montag and Fire Chief Beatty showing the chief hoarding books—he keeps them but does not read them, and therefore does not break the law. Here, Beatty explains why he *hates* books.

BEATTY
Here go the Dixie Duo, the Happiness Boys, eh?

(*He opens the door.* MONTAG *hesitatates.* BEATTY *nods him ahead.*)

BEATTY
Feeling superb?

MONTAG
Superb.

BEATTY (*to* MILDRED)
Can you count to five?

(*She nods.*)

Count to five.

(*He goes out. The door slams.* MILDRED, *motionless, counts to five. The siren starts up outside as we QUICK FADE TO DARKNESS.*)

(*The sounds fade. LIGHTS up on* MONTAG *and* BEATTY. *They have arrived at the fire chief's house.*)

BEATTY
Here we are.

Step in, Montag.

(MONTAG *steps in.* BEATTY *calls to the rooms of the house.*)

BEATTY
Everyone home?

(VOICES *murmur, whisper from all about. Clocks, stoves, radios, TVs, sound systems throughout the house answer back.*)

VOICES (*whispering, murmuring*)

Yes . . . yes . . . sssss.

Here . . . here . . . home . . . home . . .

The fireman's speech from *Fahrenheit 451* at the Colony Theatre in 1979. Tobias Anderson as Captain Beatty, Robert O'Reilly as Guy Montag. (Photograph by David Talbert, courtesy of the Colony Theatre. © The Colony Theatre Company, 2002)

BEATTY
My family, Montag. A harmless conceit of mine. I've tape-wired every damn device in my place. Assorted voices, assorted needs. Since I've no wife nor children, coming home to an empty house is better if you can call out to the TV, the radio, the phonograph, the electric stove . . . Hello!

VOICES
Hello . . . hello . . . hello.

BEATTY
And have them answer back.

Now . . . (BEATTY *moves*) . . . *watch!*

(*He steps to touch the air all about, in three or four different places. As he does so, we see in grand display huge cases of books.* MONTAG *goes into shock.*)

BEATTY
Mine, yes, mine!

MONTAG
But, you, you, YOU!

From *Fahrenheit 451*, directed by Scott Spence, Lakewood High School, November 2000. (© Ray Bradbury, 2002)

BEATTY

Yes, me, me, me!

The Captain, the Fire Chief! Makes you afraid, does it? Never saw so many books, eh? Better than that old woman's collection, eh, eh? By damn it *is*.

MONTAG *(backing off)*

Does anyone know about this?

BEATTY

Only you.

MONTAG

Me! *(stunned)*

Why me?

BEATTY

Because you remind me of the young intellectual fool I once was. Go on, Montag. Take a look. Run your hands over them, they won't bite.

MONTAG

How long have you had all these?

BEATTY

Thirty years. Oh, some of it's left over from when I was a fool. The rest came into the house after I became wise. I've brought them home, two by two, like old animals come into Noah's book-collecting Ark.

MONTAG

It's against the law!

BEATTY

Only if you read them!

(Stunned, MONTAG waits for BEATTY to go on.)

BEATTY

Don't you see the beauty, Montag? I never read them. Not one book, not one chapter, not one page, not one paragraph! I *do* play with ironies, don't I? To have thousands of books and never crack one, to turn your back on the lot and say: No. It's like having a houseful of beautiful women and, smiling, not touching . . . one. So, you see, I'm not a criminal at all. If you ever catch me reading one, yes, turn me in. But this place is as pure as a twelve-year-old virgin girl's cream-white summer night bedroom. These books die there on the shelves. Why? Because I say so. I do not give them sustenance, no hope with hand or eye or tongue. They are no better than dust.

(MONTAG has begun to touch the books with less trepidation during all this. Now he looks from them to the Fire Chief.)

MONTAG

I don't see how you can't be—

BEATTY

Tempted? Simplicity itself. That was long ago. The apple is eaten and gone. The snake has returned to its tree. The garden has grown to weed and rust.

MONTAG

Once—

BEATTY

Once what?

MONTAG

You *must* have loved them *very* much.

BEATTY

Touché. Below the belt. On the chin, through the heart. Ripping the gut. Look at me, Montag. The man who loved books, no, the boy who was wild for them, insane for them, who climbed the stacks like a chimpanzee gone mad for them. I ate them like salad; books were my sandwich for lunch, my tiffin and dinner and midnight munch. I tore out the pages, ate them with salt, doused them with relish, gnawed on the bindings, turned the chapters with my tongue! Books by the dozen, the score, and the billion! I carried so many home I was hunchbacked for years! Philosophy, art, history, politics, social science, the poem, the essay, the grandiose play, you name 'em, I ate 'em! And then . . . and then . . .

MONTAG

And then?

BELOW LEFT: Program booklet from *Fahrenheit 451,* Wings Theatre, New York City, circa 1990s. (© Ray Bradbury, 2002)

BELOW CENTER: Program booklet for *Fahrenheit 451.* (© Ray Bradbury, 2002)

BELOW RIGHT: Program booklet for *Fahrenheit 451,* Beck Center for the Arts, Lakewood, Ohio, circa 1990s. (© Ray Bradbury, 2002)

BEATTY

The usual, the same. The love that didn't quite settle, the work that wasn't quite right, the dream that went sour, the sex that fell apart, the deaths that came swiftly to friends not deserving, the murder of someone or other, the insanity of someone close, the long dying of a mother, the short suicide of a father, a stampede of elephants, an onslaught of disease, and nowhere, nowhere, the right book for the right time to stuff in the crumbling wall of the breaking dam to hold back the deluge, give or take a metaphor, lose or find a simile. And by the far edge of thirty, and the near rim of thirty-one, I picked myself up, every bone broken, every centimeter of flesh abraded, bruised, or scarified, looked into the mirror, found an old man lost behind the frightened young man's face, saw a hatred there for everything and anything, you name it, I'd damn it, and opened the pages of my fine library books and found what? What? What?

MONTAG

The pages were empty. . . ?

BEATTY

Every page! Was blank! Blank! Oh, the words were there, all right, but they ran over my eyes like hot oil, signifying nothing. Offering no help, no solace, no peace, no har-

bor, no true love, no bed, no light . . . The words were microscopic bugs, tiny islands of bacteria best burned.

MONTAG

Thirty years ago . . . The final library burnings came along at just that time.

BEATTY

Absolutely right on target. And having no job, I put in for one, Fireman First Class, first up the steps, first into the library, first in the burning furnace heart of his everyblazing countrymen, douse me with kerosene, hand me the torch!

(A long moment. BEATTY lets himself simmer down.)

BEATTY

End of my first part of SECOND Lecture. Sorry.

BELOW LEFT: Program booklet for *Fahrenheit 451,* Coastline Community College, Fountain Valley, California, circa 1990s. (© Ray Bradbury, 2002)

BELOW CENTER: Program booklet for *Fahrenheit 451,* The Wheatley School, New York City, circa 1980s. (© Ray Bradbury, 2002)

BELOW RIGHT: Program booklet for *Fahrenheit 451,* the Civic Theatre of Fort Wayne, Indiana, November 1988. This was the world premiere of the play. Cover artwork by Arthur Cislo. (© Ray Bradbury, 2002)

MONTAG
No need.

(BEATTY searches the stacks, finds a book, takes it.)

BEATTY
A little gift for you, Montag. From the old burnt-out case to the young torch-bearer of truth.

MONTAG (reads from the binding)

M ach — ee —

BEATTY
Machiavelli! *The Prince.* That'll break your jaw and your mind. People have debated for centuries about his Evil. Nonsense. He was just the grand pragmatist. Not evil at all. Take it. Start your own library of unread books. But beware. Don't read. At the very instant you so much as read one page, I shall know it.

MONTAG
Will it show in my face?

BEATTY
Always does. Readers always carry that insufferable look of "I'm smarter than you. I'm one up on everyone!" It makes my flamethrowing finger *itch*. There you go, Montag. Out the door.

MONTAG
I—

(A siren passes. MONTAG flinches.)

BEATTY
Dear me, do they know something about you *I* don't know?

(The siren fades.)

BEATTY
False alarm. Night, Montag.

(He turns.) Question?

MONTAG (has not moved; hesitates; speaks)
There . . . was a girl . . . ?

BEATTY (gazes off at some interior horizon)
Girl next door. Clarisse McClellan.

MONTAG
You read minds!

BEATTY
You'd better believe it. McClellan, Clarisse. Odd ducks, the whole family. Bright blood, which is to say, for us, anyway, bad blood. Everything we squashed in school, they grew at home. Odd girl. Didn't want to know how a thing was done, but *why*. That's always trouble, eh, bad news. Better off dead.

MONTAG
Dead!?

BEATTY
Did you know her well?

MONTAG
Really dead?!

BEATTY
Did you know her, Montag?

MONTAG
Are you sure . . . ?

BEATTY
Run down by a car. Well, now, I mean, if you walk around nights you must expect to be hit, yes? In hospital . . . no one home, except for one crazy old grandfather . . . good riddance. Surely dead by now.

MONTAG (numbed and in shock)
Surely . . .

BEATTY
Good night, Montag.

(MONTAG exits into his own darkness. BEATTY looks around at his apartment and shouts against it.)

BEATTY
Good night!

VOICES (echo, cry, shout, ring)
Good night . . . good night . . . good night!

(BLACKOUT)

7

Drawing Metaphors:
The Art of Ray Bradbury

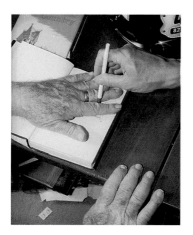

Photograph © Glynn Crain, 2001

Ray Bradbury has said time and again that the most important element of his work is the use of metaphor. Bradbury is a polymath; he thinks and creates in visual, as well as literary, media. Since childhood he has worked to develop his writing skills by passing through the "door of imagination" into a world populated by "visual myths." His fascination with film, comics, and book illustration spill over into his stories, essays, poetry, and drama as "visual metaphors," symbols, and icons.

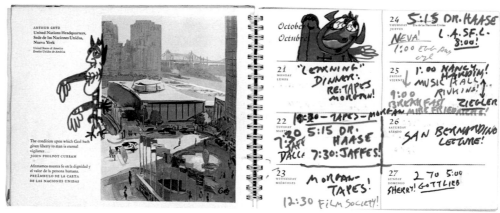

ABOVE: Ray Bradbury, artistically enhanced pages from a datebook, pen and Magic Marker. (© Ray Bradbury, 2002)

LEFT: Ray Bradbury, original painting done in 1970, gouache and watercolor on paper. (Image courtesy of the collection of Donn Albright. © Ray Bradbury, 2002)

Throughout his career Bradbury has sought out and collaborated with numerous visual artists. During his youth he befriended Hannes Bok; as a young author he discovered the work of Joseph Mugnaini, and also befriended and encouraged the EC artists of the 1950s. By the time he began to branch out into radio, TV, and film, he was taking an active role in designing cover concepts for his own books, and working with his longtime friend Ray Harryhausen to create the visual look of the film *The Beast from 20,000 Fathoms.*

ABOVE: Ray Bradbury, original artwork for cover of manuscript of *The Illustrated Man,* 1950–51. Watercolor with pen and ink on paper. (Image courtesy of the collection of Donn Albright. © Ray Bradbury, 2002)

RIGHT: Ray Bradbury, original artwork for cover of manuscript of "Summer Night," January 2, 1949. Watercolor with pen and ink on paper. (© Ray Bradbury, 2002)

BELOW RIGHT: Early drawing from one of Ray Bradbury's journals. (Image courtesy of the collection of Donn Albright. © Ray Bradbury, 2002)

Is it any wonder that during this same period he also began to paint (he had been drawing as a hobby for years)? Bradbury's paintings and cartoons possess great humor, sophistication, and a fluid, easy, unselfconscious style. Like his writing, they reveal a magical mood, a sometimes-dark comedy, and an almost primitive innocence.

Ray Bradbury, original design for "Marionettes Inc." Manuscript cover, watercolor with pen and ink on paper. (Image courtesy of the collection of Donn Albright. © Ray Bradbury, 2002)

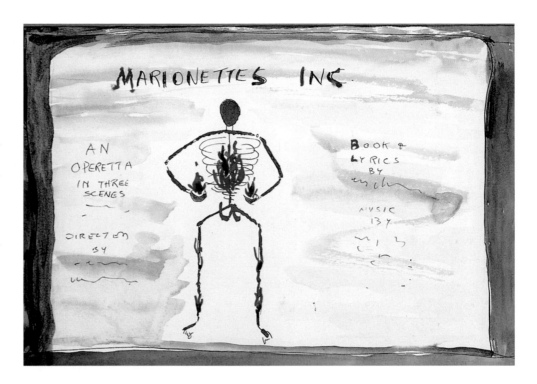

Ray Bradbury, original painting for stage design of *Mr. Marionette's Shop*. Watercolor with pen and ink on paper. (Image courtesy of the collection of Donn Albright. © Ray Bradbury, 2002)

Ray Bradbury, original artwork for cover of manuscript of *Something Wicked This Way Comes,* September–December 1961. Watercolor with pen and ink on paper. (Image courtesy of the collection of Donn Albright. © Ray Bradbury, 2002)

Ray Bradbury, preliminary book cover for *A Graveyard for Lunatics,* 1989–90. Watercolor with pen and ink on illustration board. (Image courtesy of the collection of Donn Albright. © Ray Bradbury, 1990)

Ray Bradbury, original painting of a white demon. Gouache on illustration board in wooden frame, circa 1980s. (Image courtesy of the collection of Ray Bradbury. © Ray Bradbury, 2002)

Ray Bradbury, original pen-and-ink sketches. (Image courtesy the collection of Donn Albright. © Ray Bradbury, 2002)

Ray Bradbury, original pen-and-ink color sketch for Christmas note to Donn Albright, December 1980. (Image courtesy the collection of Donn Albright. © Ray Bradbury, 2002)

Ray Bradbury, original note to Donn Albright. Pen and ink on paper, dated December 1972. (Image courtesy of the collection of Donn Albright. © Ray Bradbury, 2002)

Ray Bradbury, original sketches from the pages of Bradbury's personal sketchbook, Paris, July 1989. Pen and ink and Magic Marker on paper. (Images courtesy of the collection of Donn Albright. © Ray Bradbury, 2002)

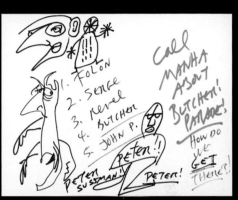

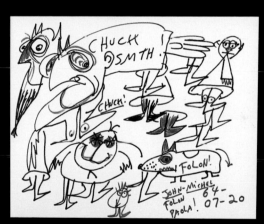

"MIXED METAPHORS"

BRADBURY - 1997

ABOVE LEFT: Ray Bradbury, *Mixed Metaphors,* original pen-and-ink drawing, 1997. (Image courtesy of the collection of Donn Albright. © Ray Bradbury, 1997)

ABOVE AND LEFT: Ray Bradbury, original sketches for various themes. Pen and ink and Magic Marker on paper. (Images courtesy of the collection of Donn Albright. © Ray Bradbury, 2002)

ABOVE: Ray Bradbury original untitled watercolor landscape on paper, undated. (Image courtesy of the collection of Donn Albright. © Ray Bradbury, 2002)

INSET: Ray Bradbury, original artwork on note to Michelle and Donn Albright, December 1982. (Image courtesy of the collection of Donn Albright. © Ray Bradbury, 2002)

RIGHT: Ray Bradbury, original untitled gouache painting, 1961. Oil on illustration board. (Image courtesy of the collection of Donn Albright. © Ray Bradbury, 2002)

ABOVE: Ray Bradbury, original untitled oil painting, 1948. This painting was a favorite of Bradbury's, and for years resided in the collection of Forrest J Ackerman. It has recently become the new cover artwork for the Gauntlet special edition of *Dark Carnival*. (Image courtesy of the collection of Donn Albright. © Ray Bradbury, 2002)

RIGHT: Ray Bradbury, original gouache painting of a fantasy landscape, 1970. (Image courtesy of the collection of Donn Albright. © Ray Bradbury, 2002)

CHAPTER 8

Bradbury at the Millennium: Poetry, Later Books, and Marginalia

Photograph © Glynn Crain, 2001

To tell the story of Ray Bradbury's life in pictures is to tell the story of American popular culture. Although Bradbury's work is grounded in a humanism that harks back to Walt Whitman and Henry David Thoreau, it also possesses a skepticism that appeals to modern readers. He reminds us that a great future is coming—as long as we are ever watchful for its fault lines.

Cliffs Notes on Bradbury's works. Cover art by Frank Brunner. (© C. K. Hillegass, 1977)

Gahan Wilson, original watercolor artwork for the unpublished cover of an all-Bradbury issue of *Whispers,* which never went to press due to publishing conflicts. (Photo courtesy of the collection of Stuart David Schiff. Used with permission. © Stuart David Schiff, 2002)

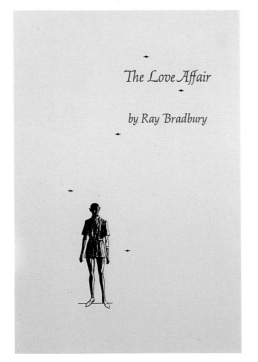

ABOVE LEFT: Joseph Mugnaini, interior illustration for special limited-edition printing of Bradbury's short story "The Pedestrian." Hand-printed by Roy A. Squires. (Image courtesy of the collection of Ray Bradbury. © Roy A. Squires/Joseph Mugnaini estate, 2002)

ABOVE RIGHT: Joseph Mugnaini, unpublished variant sketch for "The Pedestrian." (Photo courtesy of the collection of Ray Bradbury. © Joseph Mugnaini estate, 2002)

FAR LEFT: Joseph Mugnaini, cover illustration for "The Love Affair." Designed and printed by Patrick Reagh. (© Lord John Press, 1982)

LEFT: Joseph Mugnaini, preliminary sketch for "The Pedestrian." (Image courtesy of the collection of Ray Bradbury. © Joseph Mugnaini estate, 2002)

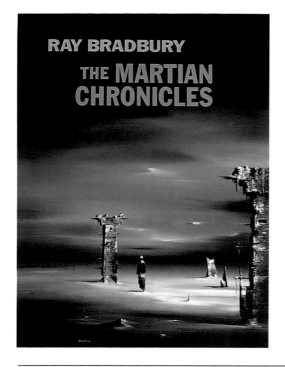

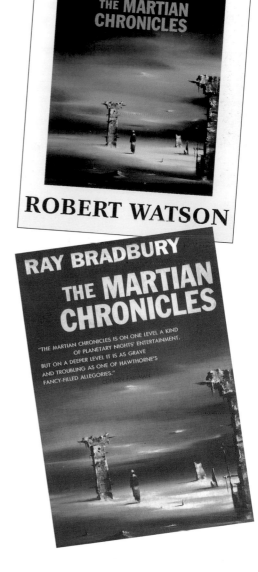

ABOVE LEFT: Robert Watson, poster reproduction of the original cover painting for the 1958 hardcover reprint edition of *The Martian Chronicles,* published by Doubleday. This edition carried a "Prefatory Note" by Clifton Fadiman. (© Robert Watson estate, 2002)

ABOVE RIGHT: Robert Watson, original painting based on *The Martian Chronicles,* from the collection of Ray Bradbury. (© Robert Watson estate, 2002)

RIGHT: Brochure for San Francisco Union Square Gallery show of Robert Watson's Ray Bradbury–themed paintings. (© Robert Watson estate, 2002)

BOTTOM RIGHT: Hardcover edition of *The Martian Chronicles,* dust jacket painting by Robert Watson, 1958. (© Doubleday & Company, 1958)

The story of his life is amazing. From his childhood in Waukegan, where his imagination was sparked by the magic words "Once upon a time," to his earliest literary output for the pulp magazines during the 1940s, he went on to write some of the greatest short stories and books of the twentieth century. Along the way he branched out into radio, television, film, comics, and theater, all the while continuing to write—essays, poetry, and, of course, short stories and novels. To Bradbury, our world and its potential are nothing short of miraculous; his vision of the here and now—and for the future—led the likes of Walt Disney and NASA to ask him for creative advice on various projects.

As Bradbury says, "We don't know why the worm changes into the larva, and from the larva becomes the butterfly. Science cannot give us the answer for this miracle, we can only observe its mystery and beauty. Mankind has always asked the question, why are we here, what is life all about? I would say that we are here to witness the universe. Without us there is no one to take the stage,

Ron Cobb, black-and-white illustration of a Martian landscape, given by the artist to Ray Bradbury, circa 1970s. (Image courtesy of the collection of Ray Bradbury. © Ron Cobb, 2002)

LEFT: Artist unknown, original painting of a "Martian Wind Ship," circa 1990s. (© Ray Bradbury, 2002)

ABOVE AND BELOW: Original covers of the magazine *Xenophile,* by Ray Bradbury collector and artist Donn Albright. These issues of *Xenophile* contained fiction by Bradbury or articles about him. (© Donn Albright, 2002)

no one to recognize the beauty, no one to probe the unknown. The universe would be an empty place without us."

Perhaps this metaphor best answers the question of how Ray Bradbury has been able to metamorphose into the creative giant he is: like the worm evolving into larva and thence to butterfly, he has refused to rest with each new achievement, and is ever reaching out to the universe.

And so we bear witness to the miracle of Ray Bradbury, an artist of word and image whose work has enriched our lives beyond measure. He has given us hope for an unknown future, all the while reminding us of the simple joys of our past.

ABOVE LEFT: *Slant* No. 2 (Summer 1949). A well-regarded early fanzine from Ireland, this issue featured a satirical story by "Brad Raybury" (written by Walt Willis), and "The Still Small Voice." (© Walter A. Willis, 1949)

ABOVE CENTER: *The Ray Bradbury Review,* William E. Nolan, ed. (© William E. Nolan, 1952)

ABOVE: *Wastebasket,* vol. 1 No. 3. Contains an article about Bradbury by Bill Morse. (© Vernon L. McCain, 1950s)

LEFT: Photograph of Ray Bradbury with Morris Scott Dollens at the Ackermansion (the home of Forrest J Ackerman), in Los Angeles, circa early 1960s. (Photograph courtesy of the collection of Forrest J Ackerman. © Ray Bradbury, 2002)

"My relationship with Ray Bradbury dates back to the early eighties, when I was publishing the book *The Dinosaurs*, by William Stout and Bill Service. My wife, then girlfriend, was a publicist for Bradbury's then-publisher, Bantam Books, and she introduced me to Ray by phone. I asked Ray to write an introduction to the book, which he generously did. My next project with Ray was the special book *Dinosaur Tales* for Bantam Books, collecting all of Ray's dinosaur stories as well as featuring a very strong original story, 'Besides a Dinosaur, What Do You Want to Be When You Grow Up?', which I had the pleasure to edit.

"That was followed by a computer game collaboration with Ray entitled 'Fahrenheit 451,' which was published by Spinnaker Software. 'Fahrenheit 451' was one of the first 'sequels' ever to a novel, and featured Montag in New York. It was produced with Ray's input and approval and was also one of the first adventure games to use 'windows'—multiple frame graphics by Robert Strong and Brian Humphries tied to the game.

"After this foray into electronic publishing—I remember taking an Atari

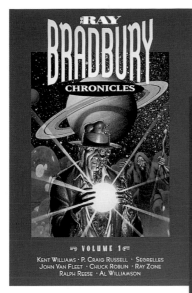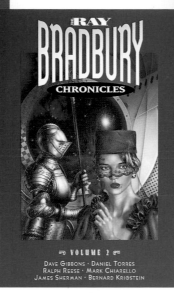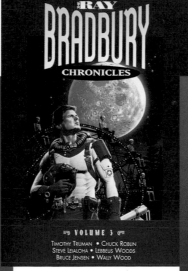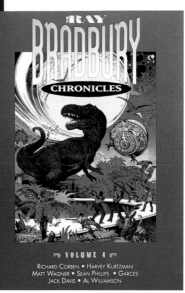

800, Sony TV, and Atari disc drive to Ray's house in a huge carrying box to demonstrate progress on the game for him—we began an illustrated adaptation of *The Martian Chronicles* for Bantam Software. This was written by Paul Preuss, a noted sf author, and also benefited from Ray's input. The illustrations were by noted sf illustrator Darrel Anderson. The game was not completed, as the Bantam Software division was folded. However, the cover art for the game was recycled as a piece for our book *The Universe,* which featured a piece by Bradbury. Bradbury also contributed to our book *The Planets,* which was illustrated with a lovely drawing in full color by Moebius.

"Which brings us to *The Ray Bradbury Chronicles,* put together by me, our editor in chief, Howard Zimmerman, and designer Dean Motter at the height of the comics revival of the early nineties. This was followed by eight additional issues under the series name *Ray Bradbury Comics,* produced by the same team and published by Topps under Ira Friedman. Collectible editions were distributed by NBM in hardcover and signed and numbered editions.

"The goal was the same from the first for all editions: to celebrate Ray's wonderful short stories with contributions by leading comics artists young and old, and out-of-comics talents like Bruce Jensen and architect Lebbeus Woods, who would bring additional range to the books. We also reprinted classic EC adaptations, which Ray loved, with permission—granted—from Bill Gaines."

—Byron Preiss, New York, 2002

ABOVE FAR LEFT: *The Ray Bradbury Chronicles,* volume 1, cover by Dave Gibbons. (© Byron Preiss Visual Publications, Inc., 1992)

ABOVE LEFT: *The Ray Bradbury Chronicles,* volume 2, cover by Bruce Jensen. (© Byron Preiss Visual Publications, Inc., 1992)

ABOVE: *The Ray Bradbury Chronicles,* volume 3, cover by Timothy Truman and Steve Fastner. (© Byron Preiss Visual Publications, Inc., 1992)

ABOVE: *The Ray Bradbury Chronicles,* volume 4, cover by William Stout. (© Byron Preiss Visual Publications, Inc., 1993)

ABOVE LEFT: "Dark They Were and Golden Eyed," art by Kent Williams, from *The Ray Bradbury Chronicles,* volume 1. (© Byron Preiss Visual Publications, Inc., 1992)

ABOVE CENTER: "Come into My Cellar," art by Dave Gibbons, from *The Ray Bradbury Chronicles,* volume 2. (© Byron Preiss Visual Publications, Inc., 1992)

ABOVE RIGHT: "Picasso Summer," art by John Van Fleet and John Ney Rieber, from *The Ray Bradbury Chronicles,* volume 6. (© Byron Preiss Visual Publications, Inc., 1993)

RIGHT: "The Golden Apples of the Sun," art by P. Craig Russell, from *The Ray Bradbury Chronicles,* volume 1. (© Byron Preiss Visual Publications, Inc., 1992)

LEFT: Original art by Doug Wildey for a proposed *Martian Chronicles* Sunday comic strip. This strip never got beyond the initial planning stage. (© Doug Wildey, 1974)

BELOW: Doug Wildey, watercolor painting *Mars Is Heaven,* for the proposed *Martian Chronicles* Sunday comic strip. (© Doug Wildey, 1974)

ABOVE: "October," transcribed by Walt Daughtery from an old recording of Bradbury reading his poem "October." (© Shottlebop Press, 1983)

ABOVE: Cover photograph for *Beyond 1984: Remembrance of Things Future*, two poems and two essays by Ray Bradbury. Designed by Ronald Gordon and printed at the Harbor Press. Cover photograph by V. Tony Hauser. (© The Harbor Press, 1979)

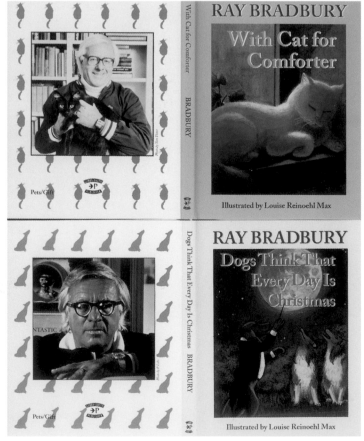

RIGHT: *With Cat for Comforter* and *Dogs Think Every Day Is Christmas*, illustrated by Louise Reinoehl Max. In these two volumes, Bradbury wrote for younger readers, as he had in 1995 with *Switch on the Night*. (© Gibbs Smith Publisher, 1997)

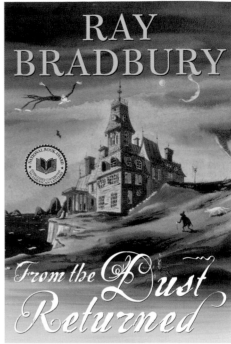

Charles Addams, title illustration for "Homecoming," from *Mademoiselle* magazine, October 1946. In 1946, the editors of *Mademoiselle* decided to build a special Halloween issue around Bradbury's story "Homecoming," and hired Charles Addams to paint the title painting. Thus began a long friendship between Addams and Bradbury; in fact, the men often talked of someday doing a book together. Years later, Bradbury's editor wanted to surprise him by finding this painting to use on the cover of Bradbury's October 2001 novel *From the Dust Returned.* Calls to *Mademoiselle* and the Addams Estate proved fruitless. When the editor called Bradbury to tell him she had tried, but failed, Bradbury said, "But darling, you should have asked me! The painting's on my living room wall—Charlie gave it to me back in 1946." And so the painting was used on the cover of the novel (although the image had to be reversed, for proper type positioning). (Image courtesy of the Tee and Charles Addams Foundation, and the collection of Ray Bradbury)

In late 1999, an Albany, New York, high school English class began a very special project. The students wrote, illustrated, and produced a book about Ray Bradbury and his novel *Fahrenheit 451.* Through this handmade volume, presented to him by Ms. Hickey's class, Bradbury is able to view his masterpiece through the lens of yet another generation of young people.

Bradbury is loved and admired by young readers across our country and throughout the world. It is fitting to end this book with an image of an enthusiastic high school class project because it reminds us that Bradbury's work continues to influence readers of all ages. And there is no doubt that this influence will endure for generations to come.

There is a marvelous mixture of innocence and wisdom in all of Bradbury's work—the joy engendered by a new pair of sneakers, the terror of the unknown, the wonder of the nighttime sky, the despair of a society that burns books rather than reads them. The most compelling aspect of all Bradbury's work, however, is its ability to transport us back to that all-too-brief time when we were young, and not yet tainted by the prejudices of the adult world. This is Ray Bradbury's greatest gift to us. With each story, novel, poem, and play he takes us gently by the hand, showing us once again what it was like to be completely open to the world around us, to the seemingly limitless possibilities of the future, and to the "visual metaphors" that surround us all.

Illustrations from a handmade book that focused on the work of Ray Bradbury, written and illustrated by Ms. Hickey's Albany High School English class, Albany, New York., October–November 1999. Upon completion of this class project, the book was presented to Ray Bradbury as a gift, and today resides in the official Ray Bradbury collection maintained by archivist Donn Albright. (Images courtesy of the collection of Donn Albright)

Yearbook photo of Ray Bradbury from the Los Angeles High School's *Blue and White Annual,* 1938. When asked to describe his life and hopes for the future (using the first letters in the words "Los Angeles High"), Ray Bradbury "spoke of myself as a thespian, but the real stunner is my predicting my future when I said he was 'headed for literary distinction.'" All this is quite incredible when you consider that Bradbury, at the time, "could not write a decent poem" (his own admission), and his fiction was not included in the *Los Angeles Annual Anthology of Stories.* We can thank our lucky stars that Ray Bradbury dreamed of being a writer, and made that dream a reality—for the stuff of his dreams is a gift that has been, and continues to be, shared with millions of readers the world over.

RAY DOUGLAS BRADBURY

L ikes to write stories

A dmired as a Thespian

H eaded for literary distinction

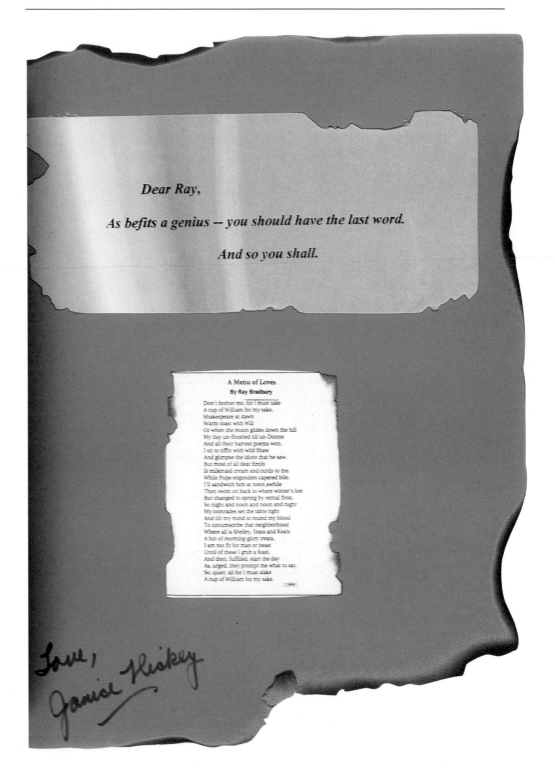

Dear Ray,

As befits a genius -- you should have the last word.

And so you shall.

A Menu of Loves
By Ray Bradbury

Don't bother me, for I must take
A cup of William for my sake.
Shakespeare at dawn
Warm toast with Will
Or when the moon glides down the hill
My day un-finished till un-Donne
And all their harvest poems won.
I sit to tiffin with wild Shaw
And glimpse the idiots that he saw.
But most of all dear Emily
Is milkmaid cream and curds to me.
While Pope engenders capered bile:
I'll sandwich him at noon awhile
Then swim on back to where winter's lost
But changed to spring by vernal frost.
So night and noon and noon and night
My comrades set the table right
And till my mind to round my blood
To circumscribe that neighborhood
Where all is Shelley, Yeats and Keats
A bun of morning-glory treats.
I am not fit for man or beast
Until of these I grub a feast,
And then, fulfilled, start the day
As, urged, they prompt me what to say.
So, quiet, all for I must slake
A cup of William for my sake.
[1999]

Love,
Janice Hickey

INDEX